SO, WHAT NEXT ?

- a look, with hindsight, at the modern world -

SYLVIE NICKELS

By the same author

The Young Traveller in Finland, Phoenix House, 1962
The Young Traveller in Yugoslavia, Phoenix House, 1967
Travellers' Guide to Yugoslavia Cape, 1969
Travellers' Guide to Finland Cape, revised 1977
Welcome to Yugoslavia Collins, 1984
Welcome to Scandinavia Collins, revised 1987
The Big Muddy – *a canoe journey down the Mississippi,* Oriole Press,
reprinted 2006

Fiction
Another Kind of Loving, Antony Rowe, 2005
Beyond the Broken Gate, Oriole Press, 2007
Long Shadows, Oriole Press, 2010
Village 21, *an anthology of short stories,* 2011
The Other Side of Silence, Oriole Press, 2012
Courage to Change, Oriole Press, 2013
It'll be Better Tomorrow, *anthology of short stories,* Oriole Press, 2014

Educational aids
Assassination at Sarajevo, Jackdaw Publications, 1966
Caxton & the Early Printers, Jackdaw Publications, 1968
Scott and the Antarctic Jackdaw Publications, 1971
The Vikings, Jackdaw Publications, 1976

cover photograph by the author: Yosemite National Park, California

To my late husband and very best mate, George

Contents

Preface : With hindsight ....

- There hasn't been a longer period of peace for several centuries, yet the world has never been a more troubled or dangerous place.

-

- Technology has provided us with the fastest and most efficient means of communication, yet there have never been more vulnerable and isolated individuals.

-

- Science has brought us the wherewithal to live longer, in better health and more independently than ever before, yet many of us continue to seek ways to make ourselves ever more dependent on technology.

-

- Advances in transport have given us possibilities to travel the world - and, perhaps predictably soon, beyond it - and yet more than ever of us remain unknowing of our neighbours and sometimes even of our families.

-

- Ease of communication enables us to pack more into each day, decreasing our attention span as we communicate with distance places while ignoring the companion at our side.

-

- Similarly, the Internet provides us with almost any information we could need, while subjecting the vulnerable and unwary to unscrupulous ways of taking their money.

-

- Increasingly, our parents look after our children and each other in the hope there will eventually be someone to look after them.

-

- Soon, if not already, we'll be able to run entire nations - if not planets - by means of technology. Equally we'll be just as capable of preventing them from operating at all.

-

- For the moment I am optimistic enough to think it's not too late to change direction where necessary. Hopefully there'll be enough of us of like mind to make it happen.

However much you think you may be prepared for the loss of a partner, unless you are a person of exceptional faith and/or resilience you probably are not. The mutual love, respect, humour, acceptance of warts 'n all that grow out of shared experiences of joy, fear, hope, hardships, achievement are privileges you can only understand if you have known them.

'My' George's life was unusually eventful. He left school to go straight into training as a pilot in Bomber Command in World War Two, was the sole survivor of an air crash, spent three years as a prisoner-of-war, many decades mountaineering, was sole survivor of an avalanche, earned himself a place on the world map with a glacier named after him - and so on. He was single-minded - perhaps to a fault. He was, he admitted, an inattentive husband and father to his children and first wife.

In several ways George and I had been linked by interests and certain experiences before we even met. I always thought that, of the two of us, I was the less dependent - perhaps because I lived and worked alone for half a lifetime. In the event I discovered that in this piece of arrogance I was completely wrong. When he fell ill, it was initially manageably acceptable as we could share in his recovery. When he got dementia and then dropped dead, it was devastating. So, in a way, writing this memoir has been a self indulgence of re-living most of the best times of my life, although inevitably also some of the worst.

Among his admirable qualities was his optimism. Even in the last months before his death when he had so many of what his doctor called 'health issues', he would ask me why I looked so worried. I suggested it was because I was concerned for his health. "Oh don't worry," he would assure me. "It'll be better tomorrow." But inevitably there came a 'tomorrow' when it wasn't better, and so I hope this piece of self- indulgence of revisiting the past will also allow George's grandchildren, great grandchildren and beyond to know more about their rather special ancestor.

1945-1950: the teens

I can't remember hearing an explosion. There's just a vivid memory of being catapulted out of sleep as a cloud of dust and a shower of debris descended on my bed. The next moment I was under the eiderdown, dragging my bear Topsy with me. Muffled by the eiderdown, Mum's voice called, "It's all right, stay where you are. Don't get out of bed!"

I heard my sister Sinette shriek "I can't see, I can't see." She was eighteen, four years older than me.

"It's the dust, darling, don't worry." Mum's voice was reassuring as it always was. When Mr. Chamberlain had told us a few years earlier we were at war with Germany, she had said calmly, "Don't worry, the war won't last long," though actually it seemed as though it had been going on forever. We were too young then to understand how it must have been for her, at war in a foreign land, away from her own family in Switzerland.

People had been talking about nothing else for ages before it started. I'd been really scared in case they used gas as they did in World War One; and because I was still only eight I didn't understand about bombs. "What happens?" I kept asking.

Dad explained that there was a really loud bang, and then something called blast would rush in one direction or another and destroy buildings. But he quickly added that it didn't happen very often. That wasn't true either - there had been hundreds of nights of air raids and trillions of bombs because we lived in the suburbs of London, but when they didn't use gas, I stopped feeling scared. When there was an air raid in the night it became a habit to collect shrapnel on the way to school and see who could find the biggest piece.

It was hot under the eiderdown, and I could feel my heart thumping and my own breath warming my face. There was a funny silence as if the house and everything else was holding its breath. By now I'd worked out that whatever had happened was due to a V2.

After the first scary experiences, we'd all got used to the V1s. You could see and hear them, so the air raid warning sounded and you would stand looking up at the sky. Their sound was unmistakable: a steady low growl. Then you saw one, black and shaped like a stubby aircraft. You'd watch it, waiting for the inevitable. Then it happened. The engine cut out and in no time the stubby black shape dived towards the earth. There would be a big explosion as it hit the ground and you knew people would have lost their homes and some probably their lives, too.

When they first came people had been really frightened. And then someone had started calling them Doodlebugs and you really couldn't be frightened of something with such a silly name. No one thought of a name for V2s. You didn't know they were coming until they'd come, and by then it was probably too late.

I intuitively knew I'd be all right, and so I was even if part of the ceiling had fallen on my bed. I pulled the eiderdown away very cautiously and looked at my room. It seemed OK, though it looked an awful mess. The window was broken, the curtains torn, there was rubble all over the floor including broken glass, some books had fallen on the floor, and my wardrobe door had blown open.

Mum appeared at the door, already dressed. "Stay where you are darling. Dad and I are checking round the house, then I'll sort out some clothes for you."

"M-u-um!" I exclaimed with exasperation. "I'm four-*teen*!"

"Yes, I know you are. We'll sort them out together then." Reassured by Mum's appearance, I tipped most of the bigger debris on to the floor, curled up in bed and called out. "Hey Sinette, are you OK? Can you see all right?" Sinette wasn't her real name but one given to her by our Swiss grandmother, and it stuck.

"Mm yes, Mum was right. The lights came on and with all that dust I couldn't see anything, but once it had settled it was OK."

Mum said we were going through a difficult patch at the moment. It was because Sinette was nearly grown up, went out with boys, and fussed about her appearance. In fact she'd had an American boyfriend for a while, who was in the Air Force. I'd rather taken to him, and not just because he gave me chewing gum; in fact I didn't particularly like chewing gum, only the idea of it. But Vance, the American boyfriend, also took the fact I wanted to be a writer seriously. I wasn't nearly grown up, not interested in boys or clothes and still preferred to climb trees, though I had to admit I was getting a bit big for it. It had been a bit of a shock a few months ago when I'd started my period, confirming I was irrevocably a girl with little likelihood of being able to be a fighter pilot, or any kind of pilot. I loved words like irrevocably, I suppose because I was going to be a writer. The period wasn't much fun either, like having bad toothache in your tummy. I'd had a secret hope that, if I couldn't fly and the war lasted long enough, I'd be able to join the WAAFs and do all that moving planes round on a big table so everyone knew where they were.

It had become clear by now that the war wasn't going to last long enough so I'd have to do something else. The main reason I wanted to be a boy was that they seemed to do so much more interesting things. Fortunately there weren't such barriers to being a writer which is what I mainly wanted to do for the rest of my life. It was really great inventing stories which I wrote out in school exercise books. So far I'd just had one or two things published in the school magazine, and in my mind I'd decided that didn't make me a writer because writers were paid for their work. So I sent one or two letters to our local weekly newspaper and when at last one got published, I was so excited. It was about all the prefabricated houses that they were putting up in the countryside for people who had been bombed out. The houses were very ugly and couldn't have been very comfortable to live in either, and in those days I didn't know anything about social deprivation. I didn't get paid for that letter either, but at least it was in a proper newspaper where other people could read it. Miss Carter, my maths teacher read it, and said if I did more homework than writing to newspapers, my maths might improve. Anyway Dad was impressed and showed it to a lot of his customers.

But what I really wanted to write were stories. My current one was now in several chapters that I'd started two or three years ago and would have been longer if I hadn't kept changing it. It was about an elf called Topsy (after my bear) and the dragon he owned, who came to find twins called Dick and Terry and take them on adventures in different parts of the world. In order to do this, they had to face anti-aircraft fire, enemy bombs and barrage balloons. The dragon, who was called Fagus, had a dip in his back full of cushions in which Topsy, Dick and Terry could curl up while they travelled. I didn't actually explain what happened if it rained. The story was even illustrated; later I tried to improve the drawings as they seemed a bit childish but I soon realised that the originals were much more appropriate to the style of writing and unlikelihood of the plot.

From my bed, I looked across at my broken window and, beyond it, to the back of the garage. Dad had a Ford Eight car which he used for getting to his shop and occasionally driving into London to buy stock. It wasn't a very attractive view but quite early on I'd found that, if I climbed out of the window, there was a way of getting on to the garage roof and then down the other side and disappearing if I'd been confined to my room for some reason.

Then I heard Mum saying sadly "*C'est 'terrible.*" When she was upset, she went back to her native French. She had met Dad on a ship travelling to New Zealand. What an adventure that must have been! I'd already decided that when the war was over, I'd spend a lot of my life travelling. Now, after a moment, Mum added, "Oh and those poor people across the road."

A man's voice responded - Mr Gregson, one of the Air Raid Precautions wardens - "Yes, most of the blast went that way. You've been very lucky Mrs Nickels. I'm so glad your family are all right. Don't let the girls come out in the front." Which immediately triggered an irresistible wish to do just that and find out why I shouldn't.

A few minutes later, Mum came back. "It is a dreadful mess out there," she said. "Our side of the road isn't too bad. But several of the houses opposite have been destroyed." I yelled out "Barbara!", and Mum said quickly that Barbara's house was fine as most of the blast had gone the other way. She also said that Mr. Gregson thought that the outside wall of my room and Dad's and Mum's room would probably collapse, adding "Anyway we won't be able to sleep in here. So we'll be sleeping in the air raid shelter for a while. Oh, and Mr. Gregson said it's been arranged that we can have our main meal in the church."

What fun, I thought, then felt a bit ashamed remembering how the lives of some people had been changed forever - that is if they still had lives. It was a huge relief that, apart from Barbara, only one other friend lived nearby, and that was in another street. That was Valerie and anyway she would be away at boarding school now. I remembered that on one of her recent holidays at home she and I had started to dig our way to Australia until her mystified mother pointed out the problems.

Now, Mum gave me some slippers to put on and I got out of bed carefully, scrunching cautiously across the debris to my cupboard.

"Why don't you put on your new siren suit on?" Mum suggested. She knew I loved wearing it, partly because Winston

Churchill had one but also because it made me feel a bit like a boy. I'd already grown out of two and the new one was still, unworn, wrapped in a bag. It was a bit big, but I preferred it like that, not wanting to draw attention to the beginning of the figure I was developing. Once dressed I put on outdoor shoes and went into the front garden. No one was about, though there were plenty of people talking down the road where the houses had been destroyed. Shocked, I stood looking at where they had been. I didn't really know any of the people who lived in them as they were all grown-ups who went to work. and their children were grown up too and had moved away. Across the road was a van where WRVS ladies were serving tea.

I wondered what I was supposed not to see, peered over the gate and saw a bundle covered with blankets. Perhaps it was a body? Suddenly I didn't want to be alone and scuttled round the side of the house to the back garden. Mum was bringing the bedding out from the air raid shelter and was spreading it out in the early morning sun. I stood looking at the shelter. I was very proud of it and liked to show it off to friends. Dad had it built quite early in the war, and it was really big as he used it to keep his stock from the shop in one half.

Dad's shop was quite small. He had a clever man working for him who was good at mending watches and clocks. In addition to this, the shop sold jewellery and china. Sometimes I wondered why he had stopped working for the big company in London where he'd worked when he met Mummy on the ship going to New Zealand. It was something to do with Grandpa who had been a bit funny in the head so Dad had bought the shop so they could work together and he could keep an eye on him. That particular Grandpa died when I was very small so I didn't remember him; Grandma was still alive but very old and a bit boring.

As well as holding Dad's stock, our air raid shelter had a small room with four bunk beds where we slept. When you were in it, all the sounds from outside - even the gunfire - were muffled. We had a light over each bunk so we could read, and a camping stove so we could make hot drinks. I thought it was great though Sinette wasn't so keen. The only real bore was that if we wanted to spend a penny we had to go in the house, and if there was an air raid on, Mum wouldn't let us, and I really hated using the chamber pot.

When the shelter was built, Dad had arranged for it to be covered by a huge amount of earth, and then planted some bushes which were now quite big and when I was younger great for playing hide and seek. Usually when we had free time I went with Barbara to the nearest park and we pretended we were a gang of which I, being a year older, was of course the leader. In fact I was quite bossy, and had talked Barbara into writing stories which we read to each other.

In the meantime, the Easter holidays were almost upon us and it was agreed that I should stay home and help Mum. Sinette, at eighteen, was at the local technical college preparing for a Bachelor of Science degree, as well as organising the taped music for the Saturday dances with boy friend Pete, the American having been posted elsewhere. I was sorry about that but Mum seemed very relieved. When Sinette was studying, I had to be quiet and that was a bit of a bore. We'd discussed whether I should go to university, but I'd decided I wanted to start work and get experience, if possible on a newspaper. So I decided to get some advice.

At the time one of the best known journalists was Richard Dimbleby. I envied him enormously and loved listening to his reports. Somehow I found out that he owned a newspaper on the other side of London, and wrote to him there. Amazingly he replied, and I still have his long handwritten letter, of which the following quotes hold the key: *Dear Miss Nickels, I have been thinking about your wish to become a journalist. First and foremost think hard before deciding to go ahead with a difficult, tiring and rather uncertain profession although always an interesting one. If you really want to do it, go ahead with the shorthand and typing..... then you get a job as an apprentice or 'junior' on the editorial staff of a local paper ....*

By the time I tried to follow his advice, shortages of paper and men returning from the Forces made the offer of my services unattractive. It was probably as well as I wasn't nearly tough enough to be a journalist; but in the end, I found other ways to follow my star.

I don't know why, but the whole event of the V2 made me think - *really* think - for the first time what it must be like for Mum being so far from her own family. A lot of children had been evacuated during the war, and I asked God really hard that we wouldn't be, and we weren't. When I thought about Mum being lonely, I gave her a big hug and she'd smile and say "*Merci, chérie.*"

For as far back as I could remember we had gone to spend our school summer holidays before the war in Switzerland, in the village of Couvet in the Jura mountains not far from the French border. We had been there right up to August of 1939 and come back on one of the last ferries before war was declared. I'd never wondered before what it must have been like to be Mum, saying goodbye to her family, not knowing how long for. In fact, Grandpapa, her father, died only a few weeks later, so that was the last time she saw him. My main rather boring memory of him was of having prayers in his room every morning after breakfast; and once he pulled me by the ear for being rude to Mum.

Before she left Switzerland, Mum and her favourite sister Agnes apparently invented a code to be able to pass on major items of news. For example, if Mum wrote that Cousin Alfred had paid us a brief visit. it meant we'd had an air raid but were fine. Following the V2 she sent a message which translated as *All well. Eating in church, sleeping in rabbit hole.* They had established that 'rabbit hole' should be interpreted as the air raid shelter, so she would have understood that we had been bombed out. The Swiss family had responded by sending a useful sum of money.

Now, the focus of the entire population was on one thing: the approaching end of the war. Everyone's head was either buried in a newspaper or glued to a radio for news of the Allies' advancing armies, minds concentrated on the thought that husbands, sons, brothers would be soon coming home. I didn't know then that they were to include my future husband. Suddenly, the war with whose anxieties and deprivations we had managed so admirably, seemed to drag interminably.

And then June 8th came V.E. Day.

"Let's go to London," Dad said. It was unusual because he hated crowds, but then those were not usual days.

I'd never seen so many people. The streets of London, which I'd only visited a few times, were packed with humanity: mad, excited humanity, hugging each other. dancing, singing, taking photographs. Many had American accents, one of whom bore down on Sinette, lifted her off her feet and twirled her round.

"We'll have none of that," Dad said, pulling her away.

After what seemed miles of walking, we found our way to the imposing sight of Buckingham Palace and stood, squashed in the crowd, round the Victoria memorial. We seemed to stand for ages. Mum, ever foreseeing, had brought sandwiches and flasks of tea. The crowds started calling for the king and Winston Churchill, a murmur growing into a roar: "*We want the King, We want Winnie....*"

Occasionally there was a movement of curtains and then, finally, a door opened and figures came out on to the balcony. There was George VI, the Queen and the two princesses who were our ages. They were distant and small but unmistakable, especially Winnie.

"Don't forget this sweetheart," Dad told me. "This is history."

And I didn't see how I possibly ever could.

----oOo----

A couple of months after peace was declared in Europe, the Americans unleashed the atom bomb on Japan: twice. V.J. Day was declared soon after. In those pre-television days we were not subjected to the horrendous reality of the effects of the atom bomb - whose results, indeed, endured long after the event. But I do have haunting memories of total devastation, of shadowy figures emerging from it, of stories of appalling suffering. Looking back, though, I suppose the astonishing fact of being at peace outweighed such horrors and it seems amazing how quickly we all got used to the idea that war was over. Rationing went on for quite a while, but among the things I remember most were the lights: the blackouts coming down and being able to see into people's houses again - probably for the first time in my case as I didn't remember much about pre-war.

The following year, just after I'd taken my School Certificate exams, we went back for our summer holidays in Switzerland. By then I was nearly sixteen. I didn't remember much about my cousins except there seemed to be an enormous number of them. Sinette and I were among the youngest. Then we were amazed by all the things in the shops that we hadn't seen for years. Everyone made a great fuss of us, and especially of Mum. It must have been hard, that first post-war visit with no father to greet her.

It was quite difficult speaking French all the time. Our accents were quite good because Mum had made us speak French during the war. We gradually got to know our cousins. I took rather a fancy to one of the girls called Nonette, who seemed very sophisticated and grown up. She was nine years older than me and worked as a physiotherapist. Her older sister Titote was a doctor and her older brother Marcel was very good looking, so I had a bit of a crush on him. Memories of what we did are a bit blurred, but I remember a lot of forest walking. Some of the forests belonged to our family and we had picnics in them and cooked sausages over a fire. Grandpapa, who had died at the beginning of the war, was a forester and had written books on new ways of developing forests. He also wrote poetry. Mum decided my writing skills had been inherited from him, though I had yet to prove I had any.

It was that summer there was another big international conference at Potsdam though I was too young to appreciate its significance at the time. Our great ally Stalin was determined to create a buffer area between the Soviet Union and Germany and it was agreed that parts of Poland, Finland, Germany as well as the Balkans would come under Soviet control or influence. It was in the following March that Winston Churchill made his famous speech *From Stettin in the Baltic to Trieste in the Adriatic, an iron curtain has descended across the continent,* signalling what became known as the Cold War between the Soviet Union and the West.

And something else really important happened that summer. Princess Elizabeth became engaged to Philip Mountbatten. The announcement was made on 9th July, Sinette's twenty-first birthday. Because of the proximity of our birth dates, we had always felt a personal affinity to the royal princesses. The royal wedding was a few months later, just before I started my first job.

On our return to England, I found that I'd succeeded in getting my School Certificate but lacked one credit for Matriculation. Not surprisingly that credit was for Science and the only subject that qualified as that in our school was Botany. I had an underlying fear of the Botany mistress - even back then fearfulness was part of my life. But you could take one subject again and I achieved the final necessary credit while I started a secretarial course at the local Tech. This was where Sinette and Pete had organised the music for Saturday evening dances, but by now my sister had moved on to the London School of Economics to complete her degree. After so many years in a small private school, the size of the Technical College was quite daunting.

Up to then, I was not aware of being interested in boys. As a child I'd developed the odd crush - as I remember in particular for Arthur Askey and George Formby, neither of them known for their good looks. And then there had been the milkman, who looked like Errol Flynn who, according to Hollywood, had won World War II single-handed. But it was at the Technical College that I was first attracted to a boy. He was called Ginger, not particularly good looking but I thought he was smashing. We seemed to coincide in the cafeteria and he usually came over to chat which became the highlight of my day. After a while I decided to write a short story about him, and it was the first one I ever sold.

At that time I was a member of something called the Society of Women Journalists and usually an editor came to talk to us once a month . The editor of *Heiress* (the successor to *Girls' Own Paper*) came one month and my story was read out. She bought it, saying it showed a remarkable insight into the teenage mind - hardly surprising as I was seventeen - and I was paid eighteen guineas, a sum I could barely imagine.

And so I launched my writing career and started my first job: as the editor's secretary for the *Estate Magazine* published by something called the Country Gentlemen's Association. The Editor, Major Anderson, commonly known as Andy, flirted with me constantly though I didn't recognise it as such as I was incredibly naive. It was during this time that I first met alcohol; a fellow worker was the daughter of pub owners in East Anglia and during a stay there she introduced me to sherry. I didn't like the taste much, but the feeling it gave me was exciting. I suddenly felt able to cope with anything, and much more grown up and in control. And after initial nausea I found I had quite a strong head.

When I got home I asked Mum why Dad never drank alcohol, and she said it was because my late Grandpa drank too much of it. I didn't understand, but it seemed better not to tell Dad about my first experiment with it. I knew that he had given up a career in the city and opened a shop so that he could work there with his father and keep an eye on him because he was ill, but at that stage I wouldn't have thought of drinking as an illness. And by the time I might have been interested, he was no longer there to ask.

While I was working on the *Estate Magazine,* Sinette and Peter broke up. She went off to Switzerland for a bit and I think went through a sad patch. Then she decided to go and live in Cambridge where we had mutual friends, and soon she had taken a job with Lloyds Bank where she met someone called Len who in due course became her husband - but not for a while.

But in the wider world, beyond my immediate horizons, events of very much greater import were occurring. Although my interest in international affairs was limited at that time, I did glance at headlines in the *Daily Telegraph* Dad read assiduously every day and sometimes discussed them with him. The first hint I got that things weren't as straight forward as I thought was when Mr. Churchill, President Roosevelt and Mr Stalin met for a big conference

"They'll be carving the world up between them," Dad muttered.

Surprised, I demanded "How can they do that? Anyway we're all allies, and it has to be better than Hitler."

"Hmmm. Not sure you can trust the Bolsheviks," Dad said. As I wasn't sure who the Bolsheviks were, I don't think I pursued the discussion. Anyway I was too busy cutting my teeth on being grown up and a wage earner, and discovering that becoming a writer wasn't quite as simple as I might have thought. On the other hand, it soon became clear that the tension between former allies was growing. Soon after the Second World War ended in 1945, the USSR began to consolidate its influence over the nations of the Eastern Bloc and enforce orthodoxy within the international communist movement by means of the Cominform.

In this they were successful with the exception of the former Yugoslavia which decided to go its own way under President Tito and adopt a non-aligned position. The latter country therefore became a major partner of the West in commercial operations, not least of which was its hugely successful tourist industry. Germany had been divided into different zones of influence: American, British, Russian, though Berlin (in the Russian zone) came under the jurisdiction of all three. The first major crisis came in 1948-49 when the Russians stopped air access to Berlin thereby starving it of vital products. In response, the Western allies began a massive airlift. By the end of the 1940s, most of the countries of Eastern Europe had become satellite states to the Soviet Union.

There were crises in other parts of the world too. India, for example, was about to experience one of the most horrendous events of its history. Though I probably was not aware of it at the time, various groups on the sub-Continent has been expressing a strong desire for independence. Perhaps the most impressive was the huge peaceful movement led by Gandhi in order to achieve this without bloodshed, and which eventually resulted in his assassination. After a long and taxing war Britain was not fully prepared to give up what Queen Victoria had called "the jewel in her crown". With huge populations of different faiths, especially Hindu and Moslem, the scene was set for terrible strife. In the end it was decided to divide the country, creating West and East Pakistan for the Moslems and retaining the bulk of the sub-Continent for the Hindus. The resulting strife probably accounted for a million deaths and the displacement of twelve million people. They are figures we might remember in the 21st century when we discuss with horror events in the Middle East.

In the meantime, back in London, after a couple of years of teaching me quite a lot about editing, proof reading, lay-outs , Andy told me to go and find a better job. Post-war Britain and the job market were changing rapidly as we all got used to the idea of peace. A lot needed to be done and so many people had died during the war that there were plenty of jobs going. Something new called Public Relations was also developing, often in association with an advertising agency. I found this intriguing and took a job as secretary with an outfit called Voice and Vision. Of my two bosses, Michael (wrote plays and was married to Harrods) was handsome and disarming, and John (down to earth) was an ex-Fleet Street man.

So I discovered public relations was a means of publicising and hopefully selling goods and services that otherwise people might not know existed or even suspect that they wanted. One of our clients was a West End hair stylist, so I had the benefit of a very costly haircut at a much reduced price. It didn't change my life dramatically but did persuade me that managing a short haircut was much easier than managing the pageboy style that I had adopted in my teens. Another client made and sold acoustic tiles, which had less obvious appeal though I could see the advantage of controlling noise in many environments. My new career also introduced me to the phenomena of press parties - gatherings to which we would invite as many journalists as possible and feed them with stories that hopefully they would find irresistible to print. We also fed them with nibbles and a lot of drink, and once again I discovered how witty and interesting I could become after a gin or two.

Another major thing happened while I was with Voice and Vision. Michael in due course introduced me to a Mr. Watt, his literary agent, and to my amazement and joy I began to sell short stories to the women's magazine markets. At this stage, it was only occasionally, but the thrill of getting a phone call from Mr. Watt to check whether Miss Nickels would accept so many guineas for her short story from this or that magazine knew no bounds. On these occasions, we would all go to celebrate in a pub. I think Michael was almost as chuffed as I was, though of course in those days you never called your boss by his first name.

Then I started being ill quite a lot. As a child I'd had a history of chest problems and the fact that I had started smoking probably didn't help. The family decided that London was not good for me and that some time in Switzerland's purer air was the answer. So I was packed off to stay with the family and perhaps look for a job so that I could stay longer.

1951-55: abroad

One part of me liked the idea of embarking on the unexpected; the fearful part viewed it with dismay. The idea was to spend some weeks in Neuchatel with Mum's oldest sister, Aunt Jeanne and her husband Uncle André, and my cousin Nonette who was the only one still living at home. From there I would go to stay with family friends by the Lake of Geneva while I looked for a part-time job.

The Swiss family was extensive, stretching through generations and across borders. It was also hierarchical. As children pre-war we were expected to run around for the adults; as teenagers we were put in charge of things that needed doing - usually in connection with family gatherings which were numerous and extensive. I remember Sinette and I looking at each other as we grew up and suddenly realising that at last we could start bossing some of our juniors about instead.

I found Aunt Jeanne and Uncle André a bit daunting. I discovered much later that one of my second cousins referred to the aunt as 'a fossil in an armchair'. This was unkind but awfully accurate. It was the sense of duty that she imparted that was so alarming because you - or I - felt this was something I should strive to emulate. However, both uncle and aunt were very kind to me, and even bought me a typewriter so I could get on with my writing. And by now I had grown up enough for Nonette to regard me as an acceptable companion. She ran her own physiotherapy clinic and owned a motorised scooter which impressed me a great deal and on which we pop-popped through the streets of Neuchatel, dropping in to coffee shops now and then. At that time coffee shops and scooters were new phenomena. I tried to write some short stories, but felt too unsettled and my underlying fearfulness did not help.

As often as I could I went to stay with my godmother, Mum's favourite sister Agnes. She and her doctor husband lived in the old family home in the village of Couvet about forty minutes away by train. My doctor uncle was pretty formidable, too, but Aunt Agnes and I giggled together like school girls, as she did with Mum, and I felt very comfortable with her. Now that my geography was better I realised how close Couvet was to what had been the border with German-occupied France. The latter had run more or less through the middle of the village of Les Verrières. When I mentioned this to my godmother, she shrugged and said, "Yes, but we didn't have bombs."

The old house in Couvet was very old, in the middle of the village, and both uncle and aunt considered by most people as *the* pillars of the community. They occupied a ground floor flat and the rest of the house was used by anyone from the very extended family who might turn up. There was also quite a large garden which required a lot of my aunt's attention. She had a couple of rather smelly dogs which we took for walks in the forest most days. I loved those forests and suspect that the family's attachment to them had entered my own genes.

"You can thank Grandpapa for the fact that they are so beautiful," Aunt Agnes said on one of our walks. And it was true - they were beautiful: not lines of trees in serried rows as some forests could be, but a natural development with trees of different sizes, as different generations had been allowed to grow alongside each other.

Aunt Agnes went on to explain, "It was Grandpapa's idea that the trees should grow up like a family, the different generations together. He called it the 'garden' method and wrote books about it, and people came from all over the world to learn about his methods."

Yes, I could see what a difference it made, with more light reaching the forest floor, encouraging the proliferation of other species including shrubs and wild flowers. Indeed there was a plaque in the local forests commemorating my grandfather for his services to forestry. Only one of my mother's brothers followed his example; interestingly, Sinette's son Nick developed a great feeling for the land and growing things, especially trees.

The time came for me to go to stay with the friends by the lake of Geneva. They had a beautiful villa, right on the lake shore. My host was a dentist in Vevey, and his wife had been at nursing school with Mum and Aunt Agnes. Apparently her husband knew everyone who was anyone in the area, including some important people at Nestle's who had their headquarters nearby. And, indeed, within a few hours of my arrival, he had set me up with an appointment to meet one of his contacts next day to discuss the matter of a job.

Everything then happened with alarming speed. Within three weeks I had been interviewed, done a test translation, and been offered a job working Tuesday, Wednesday and Thursday each week, but it had to be for no less than a year. And I had found myself a room. The way this happened was perhaps the most remarkable.

Having looked at one or two that were advertised and dismissed them for being too dark, too small or smelling of stale cooking, I noticed a building called Bon Rivage that announced itself as a *Pension pour Jeunes Filles.* Well, I was certainly a young lady. I was travelling on a tram at the time and rushed off it, ignoring the conductor who called out after me that I had not yet reached my destination, and hurried back to the large building which had attracted my attention.

The Pension proved to be run by an order of Roman Catholic nuns and the *'jeunes filles'* ranged in age from seventeen to well over seventy. My lack of religious affiliation did not seem to worry the young Sister who showed me round. She was called Sister Joseph, was round-faced and smiling and I would not have been surprised to see her sliding down the banisters. I came to call her Sister Jo. She showed me two rooms, the second of which was on the first floor with a stunning view over the lake and to the mountains of France.

Later, armed with the knowledge of what I'd earn at Nestle's and how much the board and lodging would be at the Pension, I returned to our friends to consider the situation. For three days a week, Nestle's would pay me 72 Swiss francs, at that time worth about £6, which was 25% more than I was paid for a full week in London. Beau Rivage charged 7 francs (much less than £6) a day for the room and three meals. With the comparative cost of living, I'd even have enough to carry on smoking, a habit which by then was unfortunately ingrained and which I was profoundly to regret some decades later, but then still inexpensive. At that time I was incredibly careful over money. Mum and Dad had dinned into us that you should never spend above your income and save for anything you wanted. I maintained several cigarette boxes in which I put aside money for smoking, for clothes, for trips to see my aunts and even towards any journey back to England.

Gradually I settled into my new life. My room, in its usual state of semi-chaos, was quite homely and I had acquired a spirit stove so I could make myself cups of tea. And I never tired of the view. Among the girls with whom I shared an office at Nestle's, I got on particularly well with Irene, the one translating into German which was interesting as I had retained something of a prejudice against German-speakers for a while after the war. She was lively and shared my sense of the absurd, so I started calling her Chips, short for chippy. At the pension I had befriended a girl a little younger than me called Violaine. And I had been asked by the Mother Superior if I could kindly keep my radio down during morning mass as my room was immediately above the chapel. Mum was a bit concerned that the Mother Superior might try and convert me to Catholicism, but she need not have worried as M.S. was keen to encourage me to go to the English Church. I found her pretty formidable, especially if I were coming in late in the evening when I was allowed a key to get in, which I then had to slide under her door.

But I was terribly homesick. It was an affliction I had inherited from Mum who had likewise suffered when she worked in Scotland and New Zealand. Then, as the weeks went by, letters began to make references to planned visits: letters from Mum and from Sally, the friend who had introduced me to sherry. The latter planned to travel by motorbike with her brother Harry. They were the first to arrive, in July. I had a bit of a thing about Harry who was macho but rather shy, an endearing combination as far as I was concerned as I was rather daunted by the opposite sex and how one was to supposed to interact with them.

Financially I was managing quite well. Over time I acquired some freelance translations, some from one of my bosses at Nestle's and others from one of the watch making companies that Dad dealt with. I also gave occasional English conversation lessons. Then there was the odd unexpected boost when my agent sold a short story and a cheque would duly arrive from London when I would briefly feel unbelievably wealthy. I didn't sell that many, but enough to make me feel I could call myself a writer and believe that one day I would start on a novel. In any case when you've been brought up to live within your income, it's not so difficult and at that time the expectations of the young were very much lower - not least because we'd been brought up on austerity, and the temptations that have come in the wake of digitalisation lay a long way in the future. My pleasures tended to be most closely linked with the anticipation of events to come, usually associated with visits from England or my visits home.

My notes from that time show that I became quite obsessive over whatever was the current preoccupation, usually my next or last short story, how good or bad (usually the latter) it was and the occasional outpouring of joy if I had made a sale. Even more intensive were the reactions following visits from friends or my parents, when I could express a desolation more suited to great tragedy. With hindsight it is easy to observe the pattern of depression that was later to bedevil me, but this was not a subject much in discussion in the early 1950s.

In October I celebrated my 21st birthday, at that time one of life's major landmarks. It was something of a blow to find that I had to pay customs duty on many of the presents arriving from abroad. I did feel a little sorry for myself, opening my cards alone on the day, but our good family friends had invited me round for the evening so I certainly wasn't neglected.

And, of course, there were other lighter moments. In time I came to know a few English women working at Nestle's usually quite a bit older than me. There were quite a few of them and in due course I joined the amateur dramatics group they ran, eventually taking part in a Terence Rattigan play in which I played the part of a woman with a face like a horse. I also socialised with my fellow translators at Nestle's, and with one or two fellow residents at Bon Rivage, in particular Violaine who was very mature for her eighteen years. We became good friends; we were quite alike, probably too serious for our own good, and with a tendency to work too hard which gave us an excuse to share late night brews before we went to bed. Violaine was a convinced Catholic and we had long discussions on religion which sent me researching the subject - not quite so easy in those pre-Internet days. Anyway I read enough to convince me I would make a rotten Catholic.

And then came the great news that Sinette had become engaged to this chap called Len in Cambridge whom I had never met. As Christmas and my visit home approached I became quite hysterical with excitement - indeed, it is interesting to observe the intensity of feeling that was triggered by my sense of loneliness at the time. It is true that Mum and I were unusually close and very alike and that the effect of these factors was only to deepen with time.

It was a wonderful Christmas, and I met my future brother-in-law. The significant comment in my notebook was that though he certainly wasn't particularly good looking, he was calm and thoughtful and just right for my volatile sister. He also had a dry sense of humour and a wonderful grin, which continues to remain on my consciousness long after his death. It was Len who gave me a new name. He had a slightly cringe-making habit of making puns and when I joked one day that 'my name is mud', he translated 'mud' into French as '*boue*', anglicising the pronunciation to Boo - and Boo I thus became for evermore. I also saw many friends and it is not hard to imagine the heavy heart with which I returned to Switzerland, but now armed with the knowledge that I would be returning soon for The Wedding, planned for the end of March.

My return was also tempered by an unexpected new interest. The headquarters of Nestle's, like the headquarters of any major organisation, brought in trainees for extra experience, and so I came across one hanging round a corridor one day.

"You speak English?"

I confessed I was English. "I like to practise my English. You can help me?" He was called Alex, was Swiss German and rather good looking. Happily he seemed glad to practise his English on me and we began to meet quite frequently. It was a brief if (on my part at least) intensive relationship for all of a few weeks during which we went for drives, for walks, for coffee or a drink, and in due course skiing for a week-end or two. It is clear from my notes that I did appreciate we could probably not be less well matched, but we did share a similar sense of humour and, surprisingly, Alex seemed ready to go along with my principles which, even for the early 1950s, were a bit old-fashioned. As in most things I was quite obsessive, and it was as well I had Sinette's wedding to preoccupy me when Alex disappeared from my life as quickly as he had appeared in it.

Over the months, too, and especially as we came into winter, my favourite cousin Marcel had a tendency to visit increasingly and take me skiing. He was excellent company and compensated for what might have otherwise been lonely week-ends, especially as the Alex affair (though it was certainly not that) petered out.

It was Violaine who came in while I was writing a letter home one day with a sad expression. "*Ton roi est mort,*" she announced the morning after King George VI had died. This left me feeling terribly wan. The Royal family had been so much part of my wartime childhood featuring in every newsreel and, despite my youth, I probably had a fellow feeling for this shy man who had never wanted to be king. The two princesses were within three months the same age as Sinette and me, and the thought of Princess Elizabeth taking on the huge duty of becoming a monarch made a great impression. A letter from Mum managed to make me smile, though, as a P.S. commented that we would presumable have to get used to singing *God save our gracious Queen*, and fortunately, as she couldn't sing, she couldn't get it wrong!

With great difficulty, I managed to persuade Aunt Agnes to return to England with me for Sinette's wedding. In fact, it was my uncle rather than my aunt who needed persuading. Given that domestically he was quite lost without her, he must be given credit for 'letting her go', though I suspect a bevy of parishioners agreed to keep an eye on *Monsieur le docteur* in his wife's absence. There was to be one more drama, this time entirely of my making. Minutes before our journey, I fell down the stairs at Bon Rivage and twisted my ankle. After a few moments I looked up to see the good Sisters standing in a semi circle surveying me anxiously while all the voluntary helpers did their best to stifle their giggles. In no time Sister Jo had materialised with a cold compress, the Mother Superior with a bandage, and my scattered belongings had been gathered together while a taxi was called.

In spite of some pain it was a grand journey. Aunt Agnes, who joined me at Lausanne, was a great companion and I hoped I'd be as much fun at her age. We had the wherewithal to make our own brew, and she took charge of that while, with difficulty, I clambered on to the top bunk of our sleeper. The sea crossing was good. Above all I was going home.

We were almost home when it started to snow - and it snowed and it snowed, at times reaching blizzard proportions. No one could believe it. Tom, our old gardener and handyman spent the eve of the wedding clearing the front path

For a few days, our small bungalow in London's suburbs became the focal point of visitors, delivery people, caterers, flower deliverers, telegram boys - and still the snow fell. I was whisked off to hospital for an X-ray where a doctor said I should rest my ankle and presumably it was no good telling me I should not go to the wedding. *No, it was not.* Len's parents arrived as, indeed, did half the rest of the world it seemed, including the caterers which meant shifting all the waiting guests out of the dining room and into the living room while the rest of us tried to find a vacant room in which to change. I noticed someone called Ron who had been Sinette's boyfriend for a while, but he didn't seem very put out by the prospect of her marrying. He also seemed to know his way around the bungalow and apt to take over if too many things were happening at once. Sinette showed me her outfits and looked beautiful. And for once I felt grown up. It was a lovely wedding. I noticed that Len said 'I will' well before he should have done, and the flicker of a smile on the vicar's face.

In spite of the snow, everything happened on time. The mayhem continued for the rest of the day, through the lavish refreshments, the speeches, the reading of the telegrams, telephone calls and well-wishing neighbours, and finally the farewells to the bride and groom. Before that they called me to another room and presented me with a beautiful edition of the *Rubaiyyat of Omar Khayam*. After Sinette and Len had gone and the visitors thinned out a bit, I put on a lot of records and sat talking to Ron for quite a long time. He wasn't good looking but had a good sense of humour - indeed I came to the conclusion that a sense of humour was more important than physical attraction, at least most of the time.

Soon after my return to Vevey, Ron wrote expressing the hope that he would see me when I came back to England. Alex was still at Nestle's but by now I'd decided he wasn't as good looking as I remembered and finally got him out of my system. It was around this time I began to do more cycling and also to work on the convoluted plot of a novel. My notes covered many pages and were loosely based on a complicated situation that had arisen with my cousin Titote, her sister and her doctor husband who seemed to have some mental problems. Happily I never wrote it.

I seem to have been an incredibly intense young woman. Reading through my notes from so long ago, hindsight seems to make it obvious that the anguish of homesickness I suffered then, and my need to express it, held more than a small hint of the depressions that bedevilled my later years. In view of this it seems all the stranger that I allowed myself to be roped in to a *Concours d'Elégance* - literally Elegance Competition. This involved driving a car down one of Vevey's main streets, stopping, getting out of the car, walking round it and then driving on. I had passed my driving test in 1949 and somehow found myself performing in this competition in front of Vevey's crowds. I think I wore the outfit bought for Sinette's wedding, and happily I didn't stall the engine or otherwise make a fool of myself. Nor did I win the competition and was mightily relieved when it was over.

During the latter part of my time in Switzerland, Nonette went through some trauma, and I was rather surprised when she decided she would like to travel back to England with me when I returned. Some rather wild possibilities were considered. One of them was that we should spend time in Sicily, another replacing Sicily with the French Riviera. In the end somebody's commonsense prevailed and we settled for a fortnight in Britanny.   I felt rather flattered since she seemed so much more self-assured than I was and anyway I always thought other people had more confidence than I did. It did not occur to me that she was possibly quite glad to do the journey with someone who was more experienced than she was, at least in terms of travel and languages. Presumably we booked the hotel through a travel agency who must also have sorted out the additional complexities of such a detour on a journey from Switzerland to London.

My remaining time in Vevey passed pleasantly enough. My involvements with amateur dramatics, my social life, and visits to the family filled the time between working hours and Alex featured less and less and finally not at all. By now I had become acquainted with several of the other translators' partners or boyfriends and we sometimes made up a gang to go out in the evening or on to the lake. There was also a visit from Sinette and Len. Then I decided to do a long cycle tour with a friend from Vevey to Berne. My rather prim Berne aunt was somewhat surprised when two hot and dusty young women turned up on her doormat, but graciously invited us to stay in spite of the fact she was expecting other visitors.

I rather lost track of world affairs while I was away, but did gradually absorb the fact that our former ally Russia was increasing in power and influence in the spheres it had acquired following the second World War, and that this was increasingly troubling to the Western alliance of NATO. I now also understood that, following a chequered career, the Bolsheviks had provided the foundations for the Soviet Union's Communist Party, and that their methods could be quite ruthless. Germany had been divided between East and West and although authority over Berlin itself was also divided, an increasing number of Germans were migrating to West Berlin resulting in something of a brain drain. In due course, in the early 1960s this also resulted in the construction of the Berlin Wall.

Gradually the end of my time in Switzerland was approaching. It was complicated by the fact that Sally and Harry were coming for another stay, by the need to sort out, dispose of and/or pack all my possessions for the journey home, and by the fact that Nonette was returning with me.

In the end Harry did not come and it marked the end of one small chapter of my life. He had met a young woman who was to become his wife, and inevitably the attraction of the long motorbike ride to see me in Switzerland had lost a lot of its appeal. But Sally and I had a good time.

----oOo----

I had always been rather in awe of Nonette. She seemed very sophisticated and had a presence in the way she looked and stood and related to other people. On the other hand I guessed she found it quite difficult to let her hair down and maybe it was easier for her when she was with a younger and much less sophisticated cousin. Her presence certainly attracted a lot of masculine attention, mostly from young men who were between our ages, and it was quite amusing and surprising to watch my prim cousin Nonette acting in a quite flighty way.

The first view of our hotel was disappointing, but the welcome was warm and the rooms OK - probably expectations were not so high in those days. I could see the sea from my window - indeed we were close to the beach which was huge and attractively broken up by outcrops of rock.

We put our time in Brittany to good use, visiting Dinard, St. Malo, Mont St. Michel, and exploring the beautiful rugged coast. We also seemed to pick up - or be picked up by - quite a lot of young men though their intentions did not seem to be any more risqué than to have a good laugh and perhaps a coffee or two. One to whom I had taken rather a fancy announced, on learning that I was English, that he did not like us. When challenged, he simply muttered "Battle of Trafalgar," and then became slightly amorous, putting an arm round my shoulders. With the hindsight of the 21st century it is difficult to imagine such innocence or how much was to change in the following decades.

My eventual homecoming was rather an anti-climax. Nonette barely spoke any English. Having brought her back with me, of course she needed entertaining and, indeed, accompanying on sightseeing trips into London, as well as a visit to Sinette and Len in Cambridge.

Once she had left us, it really was time I started to think of what I was to do with the rest of my life. I had kept in touch with some members of Voice and Vision, and I now learned that John was going to set up a PR consultancy on his own, and wondered whether I would like to join him. He had a large one-room office in Soho, and retained the hairdresser and maker of acoustic tiles as clients. It is unlikely that I had any serious idea of what I wanted to do, except the ever-constant wish to be a writer in some shape or form. In fact, although John and I had always got on well, I certainly wasn't the

31

hard-headed partner he needed. It worked fine for a while and was quite a lot of fun, especially when a client visited us and I would disappear upstairs to oversee non-existent staff. But in the end, I think we both agreed it would be sensible for me to move on.

Although I had not taken much notice of it, while I had been in Switzerland the Cold War had become particularly frigid in more distant parts of the world, notably Korea which had been part of the French colonies in the Far East. During that time there had been growing opposition to their rule, especially under Ho Chi Mingh profoundly opposed to the French and Japanese but supported by young Communist China. With the U.S. supporting South Korea there followed the Korean War (1950-53) whose resulting peace treaty returned Korea to its pre-War status of North and South, setting the scene for world-threatening discord into an unforeseeable future. In the former French colony of Indochina, Vietnam likewise became the scene of conflict between the U.S. and North Vietnam's Communist allies from 1955 to 1975 when North and South Vietnam were reunified. It remained a one-party Communist state but a popular holiday destination with distinctly capitalist undertones.

Across the Atlantic other divisions were just beginning to break down as black women began to refuse to give up their seats on buses to white women. .They were the first small signs of rebellion that led in the next decade to Civil Rights legislation abolishing segregation. But 1953 became notable for other major events, not least the coronation of Queen Elizabeth II on the morning of which it was also possible to announce the first ascent of Mount Everest had been achieved four days earlier by Edmund Hilary and Tenzing Norgay

In 1955, Sinette's and Len's first child Nick was born on October 9th, the day before my 25th birthday. And around that time I learned that the editor of a newish travel magazine was looking for an assistant. The magazine, appropriately, was called 'Go' and the editor was Geoffrey Portham, the husband of a lady who was French and a great friend of Mum's, as well as a fellow member of the Society of Women Journalists. It could have been a perfect job if it had not been for the salary offered. Even given the comparatively low expectations of that time, I was indubitably underpaid. However, I could see that I would learn an immense amount - and so I did.

My job description was Assistant Editor, but I ended up by doing the lot - from planning to going to press down at our printers at Ipswich. My boss Geoffrey, of course, had the final decisions.

1956-59:Going, gone...

For my generation, Europe's division into East and West happened so imperceptibly that most of us barely noticed it. Presumably it must have seemed inevitable to many after the meeting between Churchill, Roosevelt and Stalin at Yalta in February 1945, but I suppose many of the rest of us had other things on our mind, like returning to civilian life and learning to be adults. The Yalta meeting was intended mainly to discuss the re-establishment of the nations of war-torn Europe, its Declaration of Liberated Europe confirming the promise that its peoples should be allowed to create democratic institutions of their own choice. Within a few years, with the Cold War dividing the continent, this became the subject of intense controversy. Stalin broke the pledge by encouraging Poland, Romania, Bulgaria, Hungary and others to construct Communist governments. In 1956 there was a revolution in Hungary which was rapidly put down by the Russians. In a number of other instances the results of Russian heavy-handedness were overturned but none permanently until the 20th century was into its final decade.

There was something rather intriguing and mysterious about the idea of a Communist country. I wasn't to visit one before the early '60s, but before that I was to become heavily involved with another country that had had a long - and not always happy -association with the Soviet Union.

"Are you doing anything next week-end?" my boss Geoffrey Portham asked me one morning in April, 1956. Well, no - nothing in particular.

He then explained that as editor of the magazine, he had been invited on a Press trip to Finland and accepted, but now, unexpectedly, another invitation had arrived, this time to Rome. Though not of a particularly cynical turn of mind, it occurred to me that this probably sounded a warmer and more inviting offer. However, I was prepared to travel anywhere at that stage, and Finland also rang some bells. I remembered how, during the war, I had sometimes looked at Dad's *Daily Telegraph* and for reasons I couldn't then remember, Finland had been at war with Russia. The newspaper showed a map of the two countries which neighboured each other: tiny Finland and huge Russia. And it had seemed so unfair. Now I went home and asked Dad who explained that for a long time Finland had been part of Sweden, then Russia had owned it for a while and finally the Finns got fed up and, during the First World War, declared their independence, only Russia had decided it wanted it back and tried to move in again in World War Two.

After *that* war, Finland kept its independence but had to pay a lot of war reparations to Russia; one of them was leasing to it Porkkala - on a peninsula east of Helsinki - as a naval base. Our invitation to visit Finland was to celebrate the fact the Russians had decided to return Porkkala to the Finns well ahead of time. We visited the territory and saw how some of the churches had been used as stables. Apparently while Porkkala had been leased to Russia, the shutters on all the passenger trains passing through it had to be closed.

I checked the atlas when I got home. There it was: little Finland next to big Russia. And it looked quite a long way from home.

In fact it was then an 8-hour flight, which included stops in Hamburg and Gothenburg by Finland's national airline Finnair (I thought they said Thin-air at first). For the first time I heard the Finnish language spoken and found it sang pleasantly to the ear. As we lost height over Finland, I saw forests and more forests and still more forests, and the glint of water everywhere.

Our stay was only for a few days, but it marked a turning point in my life. Our time was divided between Helsinki and the resort hotel of Aulanko about an hour's drive away. It was in Aulanko that I had my first sauna, and that I fell in a love a little. The object of this worked for the tourist organisation and was popularly known as Hank - quite a bit older than me, but I seemed to prefer men that way. As was often the case, I fell for his lively mind, his sense of humour and fun, and the fact that he made me feel special. This was not a feeling I was accustomed to, except when I was with Ron and he didn't have a charming accent or that way of looking up at you from under his eyelids.

But most of all I fell in love with Finland. If people had heard of Finland it was usually because they produced good runners, skiers and racing motorists, or because of Sibelius. And then they discovered they were really, really good at architecture and modern design. But there was also something about its spunkiness and in the way it punched above its own weight, succeeded economically in spite of limited natural resources, coped with a demanding climate and a language few other people could get their tongues round. In fact they had huge natural resources but of a somewhat limited variety: trees, covering about three-quarters of the land area. Much of the rest was covered by water.

By the end of our short stay, I was thoroughly hooked, partly by Hank but even more by his country. We kept in touch for quite a while and then the relationship ran its natural course. It crossed my mind that, apart from Ron, I was getting the habit of falling for other people's husbands, but as I had no intention of getting married it felt quite appropriate, as well as no threat to the wives. Clearly this was a convenient piece of self-deception. Ron knew of my intentions and in due course found someone else to marry, at which point I remember feeling quite miffed.

I enjoyed *Go*, though I moaned like anything about our low salaries and long hours. But I had been right that I would learn a great deal - even more than I anticipated. We started off in some small offices just off Piccadilly, but it was not long before we moved to larger premises just off Fleet Street. I was in my element. Years earlier I had strolled down this iconic thoroughfare imagining some improbable glowing future in the media. Now, here I was, not with a particularly glittering future lined up, but *here* in these hallowed precincts.

My colleagues made a great team. Geoffrey's secretary Jane was sometimes opinionated but could always be relied on. Our freelance art editor Stan was a Polish Jew who had somehow got himself to the UK via France and Spain early in the war and become an interpreter before he even learned much English - I had a very soft spot for him. Tom was our cheery Advertising Manager, and in due course Philippa joined him - ex-Civil Servant, ex-Observer staff member and a generation older than me, but we became close friends for the remainder of her life. She was Jewish -racially if not religiously - and I learned a great deal from her about her race, and not least of the Holocaust about which I knew very little at that stage.

Dad, who'd had a lot to do with Jews through business and wouldn't hear a word against them, tried to explain to me about the historic Diaspora of the Jews and the Balfour Declaration whose aim was to enable them to return to areas of the Palestinian homeland in which they had lived at the time of Christ. But even before the Declaration of 1917 became a reality its future was put in grave doubt by the mayhem of re-arranged borders created following the defeat of the Ottomans in World War One. Thus were born Turkey, the British Mandate for Mesopotamia (later Iraq), the British Mandate for Palestine, the Kingdom of Heraz (later Saudi Arabia), British Protectorates (Kuwait, Bahrain, Qatar), Greater Syria and the French Mandate of Lebanon.

At different times the Caliphate, which represented Islamic religious authority and power, was established in different centres. Significantly Baghdad had been the centre of the Caliphate and thus of Islamic power and learning for several centuries; this period became known as the golden age of Islam when science, education and the arts reached great heights. Later, during the Ottoman Empire the power of the Caliphate resided at first in Edirne, then Constantinople in what was to become Turkey. The abolishing of this Caliphate in 1924 left a divided Islam at war with itself, the repercussions echoing on far into the 21st century.

It was during the British Mandate for Palestine that the Balfour Declaration finally became a reality. It read:

His Majesty's government view with favour the establishment in Palestine of a national home for the Jewish people, and will use their best endeavours to facilitate the achievement of this object, it being clearly understood that nothing shall be done which may prejudice the civil and religious rights of existing non-Jewish communities in Palestine, or the rights and political status enjoyed by Jews in any other country.

Perhaps few other paragraphs in history have been responsible for so much hope, anguish and strife. With the rising persecution of the Jews between the two World Wars, their numbers migrating to the then British Mandate for Palestine increased to the point that restrictions were imposed in 1939 - hardly, with hindsight, the best of timing. Following the Holocaust of World War Two it was inevitable that the numbers soared giving rise to increased conflict between Jews and Arabs. On the eve of the end of the British mandate over Palestine in May 1948. Israel proclaimed its Declaration of Independence, triggering an invasion by four Arab countries

Stan our Art Editor, who was also Jewish, didn't talk much about his race but taught me a great deal about lay-outs. Indeed in time we more or less produced the magazine between us, except when

Geoffrey would get a bee in his bonnet and usually cause mayhem. I was also given the task of 'seeing the magazine to bed', which involved travelling to Ipswich where our printers were *The East Anglian Daily Times.* One of their staff members and his wife ran a hotel at nearby Felixstowe where I would stay overnight. The printers always made a fuss of me and I learned quite a lot about letterpress, then the most common form of printing. But I did work very long hours.

In 1957 two major events occurred which, at the time passed me by. One was the Treaty of Rome establishing the European Economic Community (EEC) which Britain was to join in the early 1970s; the other, in October of 1957, was the launching by the USSR of Sputnik 1, the world's first artificial satellite which orbited the Earth in 98.1 minutes, marking the beginning of the Space Age.

----oOo----

Over the next few years, I re-visited Finland each summer, gradually building up my knowledge of the whole country. Earlier on, Hank joined me for a day or two and through him I learned a good deal more about Finland's history and culture. Once he came to London and it was a sign of my regard for him that he persuaded me to go to a football match. But probably the best holiday of all was in the late 1950s when I spent some time in Finland's northernmost province of Lapland. I loved its remoteness and other-worldliness, so completely detached from the stresses and deadlines of my London life.

And so one Saturday morning, sitting on top of a London bus, the rain pouring, trying to get to Stan's flat in Kensington in order to finalise the cover for the next month's edition of the magazine, I wondered what I was doing and why I was doing it. The thought of Lapland's silence became irresistible. I was in my late twenties and in the mood to do something outrageous. Then and there I decided to find a way in which I could spend the best part of a year in the far north and experience the Arctic's seasons. But I would need to earn some money somehow. Perhaps I could be a translator ... or work in a tourist office ..... or .... I began concocting a letter to Hank in my head. By the end of the week-end, I had sent it.

He replied rather quickly. *You're crazy*, he wrote, or words to that effect. But he had given the idea some thought and come up with the proposition that I could work in one or two of their hotels in Lapland and teach English to the staff, in exchange for board and lodging and pocket money. I was ecstatic. Mum and Dad were another matter. Dad, who is quite down to earth, could see a book in it (oddly I hadn't yet thought of that); Mum was rather devastated by the thought of the time and the distance, but was never likely to stop me from doing something I really wanted to do.

I decided to travel in January 1959. If I were going to experience the Arctic winter, I might as well arrive in the middle of it. Hank had suggested that I spend some months first in the sprawling village of Ivalo. This was about 250 miles north of the Arctic Circle, situated on the Arctic Highway which continued north, eventually into Sweden and Norway or, if you were in the mood to trek unwisely, through the forests into Russia. The hotel in Ivalo received year-round visits as it had Finland's northernmost airport, and it had a manageress who spoke English. Not long before my departure, an Estonian acquaintance I had made in London gave me the address of his cousin who lived in Ivalo. She was Annikki Setälä, taught English and wrote children's books.

I had never tried any form of teaching before. Research led me to some books with which you could teach English without necessarily learning your pupil's language first. This seemed to remove one complication though I had every intention of having a go at Finnish and had learned some basic phrases with the help of Linguaphone records. The lessons were largely about a rather annoying family who did all sorts of ordinary things that were boring but would be very useful to know in any language. In addition, I had English-Finnish-English dictionaries, and hoped I was properly equipped.

And so I arrived in mid-January and after two or three days in Helsinki, during which I got to know a number of my colleagues at the Finnish Tourist Association, I flew up to Ivalo. It was not as dark as I had expected. There was a luminosity from the all-covering snow and the sky had a brilliance of stars emphasised by the lack of light pollution. I looked out into the freezing, tangible silence and wondered what on earth I was doing here.

Once landed, the presence of the snow was imposing. This was not the light covering or even the few inches that I had occasionally experienced at home. This was centimetres, maybe metres thick. From the airport I took the post bus into Ivalo - the network of post buses carried mail and humanity all round the province. It delivered me to Ivalo Hotel where the manageress, Mrs Hellström came out to greet me. She was quite a formidable lady, but spoke excellent English and immediately offered me refreshment. She told me that most of my potential pupils were likely to be rather shy, but she thought I would be particularly helpful for her assistant, Kaarina, whose English grammar was somewhat erratic. I hoped my memory would stretch back far enough to the receding war years when grammar was dinned into us. In the event, Kaarina was around my age and we became good friends. I'm not sure how good I was for her grammar, but she got plenty of practice.

By then I was ready to go to my pleasant room on the first floor, do the minimum unpacking and get to bed. I awoke with the familiar anxiety that grips me when faced with an unfamiliar situation, and prayed it would go away before I had to meet anyone.

It was shortly after breakfast that Kaarina came to tell me I must go upstairs. "Today is first day," she explained cryptically.

The first day of what?

Upstairs there was a lot of chattering which went on until, quite suddenly, there was silence as the girls pointed and said a few words over and over again, which clearly meant *just look at that*. And 'that' was the sun, a tiny corner of it lifting above the dark forested silhouette of the sky line. Into the silence, Kaarina explained to me, "It is the first time we see the sun for six weeks."

It must have been there for all of ten minutes before it disappeared again.

Everyone seemed to be waiting for something more. Then Kaarina disappeared into one of the rooms and came out with a tray of glasses and a couple of bottles. "Now we say welcome to the sun," she said. It seemed an odd time to be knocking back vodka, but I noted that it was also rather pleasant and made me feel less anxious about my imminent first English lesson to the staff. During our sun-greeting, several of the girls had looked at me shyly or curiously or both. Kaarina had already hinted that I might not have many pupils. "They are timid" she said.

Yes, I'd noticed. Having given myself a crash course on basic Finnish on those long-playing records I decided to take the bull by the horns. Later I found a few of the girls drinking coffee in the kitchen, went up to them and said in Finnish, "My name is Sylvie Nickels. I would like to speak Finnish."

Or that's what I thought I said. They looked at me in astonishment, one or two mouths pursed with suppressed grins.

"You must say Suomesta, not Suomalainen. Suomalainen is ..." one of the girls struggled to express herself, then found the solution. "You see, I am Suomalainen. I am a Finn."

I grinned in appreciation. So I'd said I want to speak a Finn instead of Finnish. Still it proved a profitable mistake as four of them volunteered to come to my class in the afternoon. Thereafter I adopted the policy that if I spoke in rather bad Finnish, they would be more likely to try out their English, and so it proved.

The early lessons in my teaching books were about the Brown family at breakfast and explained their relationships, what they did, what they were having for breakfast and how they were planning their day. Mr. Brown worked in a bank, Mrs. Brown had a part time job at the local health centre, John Brown was starting at University in September after a gap year, and Susan Brown was doing her A levels in the summer.

"I know a family like the Browns," I tried to say in Finnish, and some grins told me I'd got it wrong, but at least they understood as two of them nodded and said "*Mina myöskin,*" which they explained meant "so do I".

Two more of the staff came in after the lesson had started, attracted by the laughter according to Kaarina who said she would come when she could, which really pleased me. It was arranged that I'd hold two classes, one in the morning and one in the afternoon, depending on what shift the girls were working. They were held in one of the smaller lounges on the first floor, normally used in the evening for pre-dinner drinks and nightcaps. As the days passed and the sun became larger on the horizon, I began to feel I belonged in this strange, lonely place. The girls began to try out a few words in English on me, indicating that they were actually doing a bit of homework, and likewise I tried out my Finnish on them.

One or two of them invited me to their homes, or to join them in the sauna. It still seemed a bit strange socialising in my birthday suit, but my final triumph was when I literally took the plunge: after sauna going out on to the frozen river to descend a small ladder into the freezing water. They actually cheered me as I hurried back to the sauna afterwards and then gave me a rather large glass of rough brandy as a reward. In fact I soon learned that the Finns were quite partial to their alcohol. It became quite a regular event that Kaarina and I would have a nightcap or two before retiring, often joined by friends of Kaarina who quite often visited from the nearest small town of Muonio. It was as well I didn't have much spare money or I might have been drinking more than was sensible even earlier than I did.

It was soon after the frozen-river episode that I decided to make contact with Annikki Setälä. She was well known in Ivalo and, armed with precise instructions, I set off down the Arctic Highway. It was well into the evening, but the combination of snow and stars provided more than enough light.

I knocked on her door, heard movements within, and then the door opened. A woman in her fifties with a pleasant, enquiring face surveyed me. "*Molim?*" she said, which I knew was the common greeting of enquiry, equivalent to 'can I help you?'

"I am a friend of your cousin Hillar," I said.

"Ah, Hillar!" Annikki Setälä said. "Please come in and take coffee with me."

While she prepared the first of many thousands of coffees we were to share together, she went on, "Yes, Hillar wrote to me. He says you are a writer. How is he? How long are you staying? Have you been to Finland before? What kind of things do you write?" It was my first experience of Annikki's tendency to say everything that went on in her head at once. This time, though, she stopped and added wryly, "I ask too many questions. We shall talk over coffee."

And so we did and I fell for the disarming openness which no doubt contributed towards making Annikki such a successful children's author. Indeed, there was something child-like about Annikki herself.

So I learned that she taught English in the local school, which included quite a few Sami or Lapp children. It seemed in this area, the Sami did not follow the reindeer herds throughout the year, as they once did. They built their own homes and lived in the community for the winter, then followed the reindeer up on to the fells where the herds would graze during the summer until they were collected and brought down again in the early autumn.

"I think there is a ... a *poronmeritys* ... a reindeer round-up happening soon not far from here. Perhaps you could go with the family of one of my girls - I mean one of the Sami girls I teach,"

"That would be wonderful," I said.

"I wish I could go with you, but I have to go south to see one of my girls." She was divorced but apparently had three daughters, all a little older than me.

We talked about her family, and about the war. I had already learned how difficult it was to be on the 'wrong' side - that is, allied with Germany who was fighting against our allies, the Russians.

Towards the end of the war, the Germans were obliged to evacuate from Finland where many of them had been stationed. In the process they had razed most Lapland communities, including Rovaniemi, to the ground. I'd already visited Rovaniemi, the capital of Lapland province and situated pretty well on the Arctic Circle. It had been completely re-designed since the war, largely by Aalvar Aalto, one of Finland's leading architects. I told her about my memories of the maps of little Finland and big Russia in Dad's newspapers.

Annikki smiled. "I think we shall be good friends," she said. And I thought so, too.

I also learned that Annikki owned a small island off the south-west coast of Finland and spent a lot of the summer there. I'd never met anyone who owned an island before and thought it would be a wonderful thing to do.

It was sometime later on my way back to the hotel that I wandered a little further along the road where it crossed the river Ivalo. As I stood leaning on the bridge balustrade, something made me look up. Above me was a sight of such magic I could only stare and stare at the veils of colour - green, rose, yellow, that shifted and parted and met and swirled. At times they seemed to move towards the horizon as though they would disappear, but suddenly they were re-ignited somewhere else and took on a new life. Suddenly I was aware my mouth was open and closed it. So these were the famous northern lights! I'd seen traces of them before, but never such a stupendous display. I felt a sense of completeness I had not felt for a long time.

A few days later, Annikki came to the hotel to tell me she had arranged with Inge, the schoolgirl daughter of one of the Sami herdsmen, to take me to the reindeer round-up. She was fifteen, shy, but had been chosen because she was top in class for English, and was clearly enormously proud of her responsibility. And her English was amazing in more ways than one. I'd learned by then that Finnish was not an Indo-European language but belonged to a smaller linguistic group along with Hungarian and Turkish. This meant that it was phonetic and therefore relatively easy to pronounce, but with a grammar that bore no resemblance to any other Western language. So, I now knew that *Suomi* meant Finland in Finnish; *Suomeeen* was 'to Finland', *Suomesta* from Finland, and *Suomesta* was also the partitive case which it took me a long time to sort out. Small wonder that Inge's English was a little quaint.

She tried to explain to me what would be happening at the round-up. "So the men bring the reindeer to the reindeer round-up and that is where they .are...." she looked a bit helpless again. But together, with the help of the dictionary we worked out that the reindeer would be divided up: according to their owners, then according to whether they would be trained as draft animals, or killed for meat, and especially the young calves born from the last time would be selected and marked by cuts in the ear to identify their owners.

It was about an hour's drive and then half an hour on skis, fortunately along a wide, level track. My skill with skis was still unpredictable when it came to downhill, but cross-country was manageable as long as I could take my time. We could hear the shouts of the herdsmen and the grunts of the reindeer long before we reached the site.

It was arranged that we should sleep in a *tupa*, a wooden hut of which there were several. It was the name given to such huts which dotted the fells and were available for any passerby to spend the night, provided they left it in good condition and replaced any logs they had used for a fire. We left our belongings in the *tupa*, bagging two places in one of the smaller bunk rooms. When it came to spending pennies there were outdoor loos serving the huts; otherwise, you just headed out into the forest and hoped you wouldn't be stumbled upon. I'd been provided with a pair of reindeer skin shoes, stuffed with special grass for warmth; very cosy they were too.

Someone had lit a fire and a very old Sami woman was boiling water over it in a copper kettle. She was dressed in the colourful traditional dress as so many of them were, and invited us to have a cup of coffee with her. She was clearly curious about me and I left Inge to explain who I was.

"She is very surprised you have come so far," Inge translated. "For her England is like another world."

Yes, well I could relate to that. The coffee was particularly good, and Inge and the old lady went on conversing while more people arrived, most of them needing an explanation about me.

It proved to be a memorable day, quite 'other' compared with any that I had experienced before. The reindeer had already been brought in and were in a very large paddock from which they were herded in smaller numbers into the confines of a corral. This was divided into two; their owners lassoed them one by one and pulled them from one to the other. They then examined them, marking the young ones that had been born since the previous round-up; making a decision as to which would be sold for meat; and doing something unspeakable to a few that would be trained for transport. This was beyond Inge's English but I guessed correctly they were being castrated in order to make them easier to train.

It was bitingly cold. A lot of the reindeer people had brought vodka or a cheap kind of brandy to keep the iciness out, and were generous in sharing it. I didn't refuse it. It didn't strictly speaking keep the cold out, but it certainly made you feel warm inside. When they finally got back to the *tupa* for the night, my reservations about such communal sleeping returned but, in the event, I shared with Inge and her very extended family. There was no question of undressing or washing and I just assumed you couldn't get very dirty in such an intensely cold and unpolluted setting. Anyway I need not have worried. Bottles of something strong were liberally being passed around and I almost fell asleep mid-sentence.

Next morning Inge said, "My uncle asks would you like a reindeer ride?"

Truth to say I was suffering a bit from a hangover and wasn't too sure.. However, as I'm usually game for anything and assumed I wasn't expected to ride on the reindeer's back, I nodded, and Inge explained, "It will be in a *pulkka.*"

"Is that a sledge?"

"A sort of sledge, a small one. It is like a kind of boat. Come I will show."

She was right. It was a bit like a boat, a stubby canoe. I got in and they tucked several reindeer skins round me. It was a relief to see that Inge's uncle was coming too, driving the lead reindeer pulling a proper sledge on which Inge rode. He set off at quite a pace, and I waited for mine to follow, but it just stood staring down at the snow.

Inge called back, "You must let him go!"

"I'm not stopping him," I protested a trifle woozily. For a start, I wouldn't know how. Eventually one of the other reindeer herders came over and issued the reindeer with some instruction which prompted him to follow the leader. After a few moments, I was able to snuggle under the reindeer skins and enjoy the sheer wonder of the experience: the biting cold, and the beauty of the forest enveloped in layers of snow that muffled all sound.

And there was to be yet one more treat. That evening, the Aurora was especially beautiful. Kaarina had told me there was superstition that if you whistled at the lights they would come down and take you, so I thought *perhaps I will try to whistle at them, and see what happens.* I looked up and whistled gently. Nothing happened and it's probably wishful thinking, but some years later I found myself wondering whether, indeed, that whistle had not triggered something unexpected that was to happen before too long.

----oOo----

And then one day Mrs Hellström told me, "Helsinki have decided that it would be a good idea if you spend the rest of your time in Lapland at our hotel in the western fells: at Pallastunturi. It is a beautiful place and you will like it."

This turned out to be a solitary place with stunning views and was at the beginning of a hiking trail that led through the wilderness to a village some sixty miles away. I became particularly good friends with the manageress of the hotel called Johanna, whose English was good if the grammar a little quaint. We did the hiking trail a couple of times, stopping overnight in wooden cabins where you could sleep and light a fire. Manu, her Dachshund went everywhere with us, usually running three times the distance that we walked, and completely revising my opinion of sausage dogs. Indeed, I was so taken with him that on my return to England I acquired a Dachshund myself, naming him Pilkku (Finnish for 'comma')

"He is the light comma of my life," Johanna had asserted early on. I worked out that she meant 'bright spot'.

Johanna's assistant Eva also became a good friend and she and I often went out on more local walks when she was off duty. She was a great flirt and it was her custom when we came within sight of the hotel to pause and say "So, how many cars?", then, "and how many men?"

While I was in Pallastunturi, I met Johanna's young friend Matti, a student at Helsinki University who had just completed his finals on the curious combination of botany and traffic problems. It was a fun time as Matti's English was quite good and he was rather handsome. Together with a visiting member of the Finnish Tourist Association, we went on a fishing expedition, when, under the midnight sun, I achieved my first ever catch. Matti and I arranged to meet up in Helsinki, where he introduced me to his equally good looking girl friend and the three of us have remained friends ever since.

By now I had made a firm decision to write a young people's book on Finland. One of my travel writing friends was married to a publisher of books for young people, including a series on foreign countries and I approached him with a synopsis for book on Finland which was accepted. The fact was that, on my return to Fleet Street, I found that *Go* had 'gone' - or rather it had been taken over by a very rich young entrepreneur to whom I had taken an instant dislike. I therefore decided to make a serious effort to live by freelancing and became self-employed - perhaps under the illusion that it was rather easier than it turned out to be.

Looking at the records for my output and income during those early years, it certainly was not easy. I had regular sales to a Finnish publication, to UK travel trade magazines, The Lady, occasional sales to a national newspaper, and to publications which no longer exist and (most rewarding of all) short stories in various women's magazines. And I was working on that first book for young people.

By the time I returned to England, major world events were unfolding, this time rather far away in the Far East again and, as yet, not leaving a great impression on my mind. This was the re-lighting of the Vietnam War, a more distant version of our Cold War in the struggle between the West (supporting South Vietnam) and Communism (supporting North Vietnam). It was to drag on for twenty years resulting in millions of civilian and military deaths and displaced persons, at times violently opposed even in the U.S. itself.

Soon after my return to England, I also became an aunt for the second time with the birth of my niece Claire on October 7th,1959, three days before my29th birthday and two days before Nick's 4th. The world, it seemed, was becoming full of Librans.

Then something else occurred which was to affect the rest of my life.

1960s: life changes

It was March, 1960. There was nothing about the envelope to signify anything dramatic. Once opened, I was first struck by the letterhead: SOUTH GEORGIA HIMALAYAS LAPLAND, and below it was an address in Kendal in the Lake District. I read:

"Dear Miss Nickels - I am writing to you at the suggestion of the Director of the Finnish Tourist Association in London who feels you may be able to offer me useful advice.

You will see from my notepaper that I am a lecturer and photographer, and I have chosen northern Scandinavia as the scene for my next talk. I have already spent some months in the area alone last year, largely in Norway and Sweden, mountaineering and fishing combined with long cross-country treks. I am returning to Lapland this summer and again in the spring of next year and most of the time will be spent in northern Finland.

As a writer I am sure you will know the kind of material which goes to make a good lecture and I am wondering if you have any particular suggestions to make. If you can make any recommendations either with regard to the Lapps or any other subject which you think would be of interest I should be most grateful.

I should be particularly pleased if we could meet......"

It was signed 'George B. Spenceley, Photographer, Lecturer. I read it again. How intriguing.

I spent a lot of time answering George Spenceley's letter, and there followed a further short exchange before he wrote to say he was lecturing near London and he hoped he could take me to lunch. It was agreed that we should meet outside the Dominion Theatre in Tottenham Court road, each carrying a copy of *The Times*. I arrived a little late, displaying my copy of the newspaper a little self consciously and, when no one accosted me, went to look at the photographs advertising the current film. And then a voice said "Miss Nickels?" and I turned to see a pleasant-looking man in his forties with an enquiring expression. In response I held out my hand.

Later George told me that if I had not seemed interesting, he would have taken me to a cheap little Italian restaurant he knew, but otherwise we would go to Kettners in Soho, a particular favourite with the climbing fraternity. In due course I got used to George's brand of flattery; it went with his skill at giving good lectures. Anyway, we went to Kettners.

We talked and talked. Initially it was about Finland and George's lecture, exchanging experiences, while I enlarged on suggestions I'd made. George was going to northern Finland for Easter and planning to follow my recommendation to attend one of the Sami wedding festivals held at that time. By coffee time, we'd moved on to other areas of our lives. It was then that I learned of George's experiences during the war.

"Oh, I so wanted to be old enough to join the R.A.F.," I said.

"Well, I can tell you that Bomber Command wasn't a lot of fun," George said. "Though in a strange way the danger was almost addictive. You felt so elated when you got back and realised you'd survived that you wanted to do it all again. All the same, I guess being shot down saved my life - I'd already outlived the number of ops that most pilots survived."

"You were shot down?"

"Mm. And the sole survivor. It was a scratch crew in one of those huge raids they started in 1942. So I was rear gunner for the first time - and that saved me – though I had a fractured skull." He pointed to an impressive long dent near his hairline.

"You sound like a cat with nine lives!"

George grinned. He had a very nice grin. "That's what Adrian is always telling me - my second son. He's always been a bit precocious, but now he's in his teens, of course, he knows it all. His first brother Julian is rather more introspective; perhaps too much so. It'll be interesting to watch developments. Nick, the third one, is showing signs of being bookish." He sounded pleased.

Ah, three sons. Obviously, a wife too.

"So what about your war?" George asked.

"I was at school and didn't really have one. Well, there were a lot of air raids, and then the V2 that just missed us a few weeks before the end of the war. I used to collected bits of shrapnel on the way to school. Oh and I did write a poem and sold it for War Weapons Week - and collected £4. 15s. Dad got it printed for me and I sold it at tuppence a time."

"I was on leave during some bombing raids early in the war. I thought they were terrifying. But those V2s must have been the worst, I imagine, because you couldn't see them coming."

"More terrifying than being shot down?"

"In some ways. I woke to find myself surrounded by women in long gowns, and thought I'd gone to heaven." Again that attractive grin.

"Was your wife in the war?"

George hesitated. "She was a teacher. In fact, I met her just a few weeks before I was shot down." He started to say something else, then changed his mind and asked, "And you, do you have any commitments?"

I shook my head. "I really want to travel and write. I'm freelancing at the moment. In fact, I've just finished working on my first book: on Finland! It's aimed at children."

"That's amazing," George sounded genuinely impressed. "I think you're the first author I've met. I imagine it's quite difficult making a living from writing?"

"Yes, it is, though I don't really think of myself as an author yet. And what about lecturing?"

"It would be if it was all I did. But I'm a full time teacher as well. So it helps to pay for my climbing trips and occasional expeditions."

"How on earth do you remember it all?"

"Aaahh, that's a professional secret." After a while he gave in. "The truth is that there is no way I could remember all the facts, and I think looking down at notes looks a bit amateurish. So, I learn in what order the slides are so that I don't have to look back and check. Then each slide acts as a memory-jogger as to what I need to say next." He looked a bit sheepish. "And if I do hesitate, it makes it seem more authentic."

"You mean you're acting!"

"Yes, but it's all true. You'll have to come and listen one day."

"Mm, I hope I shall. So what does your wife think of your globe-trotting?"

George grimaced "Well, I've been a pretty neglectful husband and dad, so not a lot. I'm pretty selfish about it, I suppose. But I reckoned I'd missed out on being young during the war and am trying to make up for it. Well that's my justification anyway."

I nodded. "I suspect that's probably why I find it difficult to commit to a relationship. Not that I missed out on my youth. I thought the war was a big adventure. But I've always wanted to travel. My mother met my father on a ship to New Zealand so I guess the travel bug was built into my genes. It's difficult to commit if you're on the move the whole time. Or perhaps it would be more honest to say that I prefer the moving to the committing."

"Well, it would also depend on to whom you were committing. They think very highly of you at the Finnish Tourist Association. They said you were planning to go back next year too."

"That's right. I'm thinking of doing a guide book, and I have quite a few gaps to fill. Who knows, we might bump into each other."

But I was totally gob-smacked when we did.

----oOo----

After I'd done my research the following summer I headed north for Pallastunturi, Johanna and her 'light comma'. I chose early June because the mosquitoes were less bothersome before midsummer. We had a few days talking and talking, and walking on the fells. And then one afternoon, returning from a solitary walk, I was amused to see a reindeer standing by the entrance to the hotel, and beside it, leaning forwards towards it as if in conversation, a familiar and unexpected figure.

"*Tervetuola Herra Spenceley*!" I greeted it.

"*Kiitos, kiitos*," George returned. Dressed in trekking clothes, he looked quite different from our last meeting. "Those are two of the few words I have learned - welcome and thank you. But I didn't dare hope we would actually meet." He paused and looked a bit sheepish. "In fact, we might not have done if I hadn't burned down my tent."

I raised questioning eyebrows and George continued, "My pipe. I thought I'd put it out, but it was smouldering and sort of sparked off a fire so..."

"No tent?"

"No tent, but fortunately I'd left most of my gear outside as it was such a fine night, and managed to get out with my sleeping bag before I lost that, too." He grinned. "It was a very stupid thing to do."

"It was."

"Happily the tourist association said I could get a bed at any of their hotels in case of need."

They had moved up the steps into reception. Johanna was talking to some guests and turned. "Ah you have found your countryman, Sylvie. He has had an adventure."

I corrected her. "No, he's been stupid."

Johanna chided "It is not kind so to say," and I grinned to show I wasn't serious.

I went to wash and change and then joined George in the small first floor lounge for a drink. We exchanged news - my research tour, and his considerable trek across from northern Norway into Finland. Apart from the fire it had been a great success and he was pleased with the variety of slides he had for his next lecture.

"So when are you going home?" I asked.

"Pretty soon. Our climbing club is going to the Alps in August and I've a lot of preparation before school starts, so I think I'd better show the family they still have a husband and father." *Yes*, I thought, *that might be a good idea*. "To be more precise, I'll leave in two days' time. Perhaps tomorrow we could have a day on the fells."

"Sounds good. Though you may have to moderate your pace."

It proved to be a memorable day. There was so much to talk about, so much to look at, a grand picnic prepared by the kitchen staff, so I didn't have to worry about the pace. We had our picnic on top of a fell called Pyhätunturi which meant Holy Fell. Over coffee we fell silent gazing out over the hugeness of rolling landscape that was Lapland. Neither of us spoke for a long time, completely absorbed by our surroundings. Then into the silence, George said "I wish I'd met you a long time ago."

Oh, I hadn't expected that though I'd been thinking how very pleasant it was to have a day with such a compatible companion. "It probably wouldn't have worked," I said at last. "I think we're both too selfish."

"I wouldn't have needed to be selfish with you," George said. Before I had time to anticipate it, he suddenly leaned across and brushed his lips across mine. Then said, "Sorry, that was presumptuous."

"It was a bit," I agreed, though it had been rather pleasant.

Perhaps it was as well he was leaving the next day. All the same, I got up to see him off on the early bus, and as he got on to it leaned up to kiss him on the cheek.

"You like this Mr Spenceley," Johanna observed as I returned to the hotel.

"He's married," I said.

"Yes," Johanna said. "I'm going in to Rovaniemi after breakfast. Would you like to come?"

----oOo----

"It's been a long lonely summer," Mum said when I eventually got home.

51

I felt a twinge of guilt. "Sorry, Mum. I was getting on so well with the book and it was so ... it felt so right up there in all that space. And then I met up with that young couple I told you about." I could well understand that it must have seemed a long summer. Dad was great but he was so absorbed in his small business where he spent all day, and then most of the evening working at his desk on accounts or planning the next intake of stock.

"And you met that George Spenceley again," Mum said shrewdly.

"Only for a couple of days. It was really nothing to do with him." Later I found myself questioning that statement. Of course, it was grand having a companion with whom I had so much in common. And since I'd arrived home I'd noticed how many of my own circle had acquired permanent partners, one or two even married, and a couple with babies. Not that I was a great committer. Anyway George Spenceley was well and truly married and, I suspected, not a great committer either.

A few days later a letter arrived from him. ".... it was a real curse that I couldn't stay on in Pallastunturi, but I had to get back for that Club meet as well as start on my new lecture, and I suspect I might not have got much work down if I had stayed on." He ended by saying that he would be coming south for a couple of lectures in Essex and wondered whether we might meet.

I announced at breakfast, "George Spenceley has some lectures in Essex in November. Could he come and stay here? Then you'll see how civilised he is. He won't be any trouble as he always takes his sleeping bag everywhere with him, usually sleeping in the car."

Mum didn't hesitate. "We can at least offer him the sofa. We'd both be pleased to meet him."

As I'd anticipated they were both impressed by George's courtesy and good manners. Well, it must have made a pleasant contrast with some of the young men I'd brought home. Of course, George was also more mature. In fact, most unusually Dad abandoned his desk for the evening and commandeered George's attention while questioning him about his time in Bomber Command.

"Sorry about that," I said when my parents eventually went to bed.

"Not at all. He's a splendid man. They're both splendid. I adore your mother."

52

But it was in the early 1960s that we had to face the fact that Mum's health had seriously deteriorated. She had been diagnosed with diabetes a good while back, and we had dealt with the complexities of establishing she needed insulin but was allergic to it. At that time the sources of insulin used were from the pancreas of beef or pig. After many trials it was found she could tolerate a particular Danish insulin made from pig's pancreas . Nevertheless, she still suffered from attacks of hypoglycaemia, when the insulin didn't work properly and the resulting lack of sugar gave her funny turns that could only be reversed by plying her with a sweetened drink.

It was also in the 1960s that I had acquired my own Dachshund called Pilkku, had enjoyed his company for three years and then had to have him put down. Our nice vet was angry. "They breed them longer and longer without thinking of the consequences," he fumed. In Pilkku's case he stopped being able to pee and after one operation it was not possible to do anything more and we had to have him put down. After a while we acquired a mongrel cat and named her Sappho.

. The 1960s saw great changes throughout the world and even beyond, notably with the intensifying race between the US and USSR as the Space Age developed. In the mid '60s, the Soviet Union managed a Space walk and the US the orbital docking between two spacecraft. Now almost taken for granted, it then seemed more like science fiction than reality. But pre-dating the Internet, even major events did not co-relate as they were to when the world was linked by a few clicks of a mouse. In 1962, the Cold War became very dangerous indeed though in this case it was not on our European doorstep but away in the Caribbean.

Following a failed U.S attempt to overthrow the Communist Castro regime in Cuba, the latter entered into an agreement with the Soviet premier to place Soviet nuclear missiles in Cuba. As tensions grew over several months, the world held its collective breath. In October, when the prospect of a nuclear holocaust seemed nigh unavoidable, a mutual backing down of Presidents Kennedy and Krushchev allowed us all to breathe again. By then, alarmed by the 'brain drain' from East to West Berlin, the Soviet Union had demanded the withdrawal of Allied troops from West Berlin and when this was refused began building the Berlin Wall in 1961which was to divide the city for thirty years.

It was in the same year that I visited my first Communist country and began to specialise in Eastern Europe. It happened this way. One of the regular contributors to *Go* magazine had been Gordon Cooper, an older man very well established as the author of a series of popular travel books aimed at a post-war readership who by now took it for granted that they could go abroad for their holidays. The series was called *A Fortnight in ....* and Gordon had written one for just about every popular holiday destination of that time. We had always got on well and now he approached me to ask if I would be his assistant - researching subjects, taking his place on press trips and generally relieving him of some of the increasing burden that had come in the wake of his success. He also wrote regularly for the *Sphere* magazine. He lived in London so my regular visits to his flat were the equivalent of going into the office.

Quite soon after I began working for him, he asked if I would represent him on a trip to what was then Yugoslavia. It would mean a few days in the mountains of Slovenia, and a few more in Sarajevo, the capital of Bosnia-Herzegovina. Of course I leapt at it, and this was another event that had a major effect on my life. I knew very little about Yugoslavia except that it was a Communist country but kept itself independent from the influences of the Soviet Union. I arrived by rail and remember peering intently out of the window as we crossed the border, presumably expecting some major change to accompany the occasion. But all I saw were Slovenia's splendid mountains looking very much like those of adjoining Austria.

In Ljubljana, Slovenia's capital, I was met by a tourist guide. In due course I moved on to Sarajevo, capital of Bosnia-Herzegovina, which could not have been more different. Thus I learned that Yugoslavia was made up of six republics which, for centuries, had been divided from each other, about half under the rule of the Habsburg Empire and the other half under the Ottoman Empire. During that period half of them used the Roman alphabet and tended to follow the Catholic faith; and the other half used the Cyrillic alphabet and followed either the Orthodox or Moslem faith. In fact, Yugoslavia had been one of the results of the break-up of the Habsburgs and Ottomans after the First World War. It began as a kingdom then, after World War Two, had become a Communist Federal Republic under President Tito. The first republic to become independent that had been under the Ottomans was Serbia, and most of the Serbs retained their

Orthodox faith. I found this mix fascinating and studied it closely over the following years.

Indeed it is curious that, from time to time, you come upon a place you have not visited before and immediately feel at home there, even though you do not speak the language or, in the case of Bosnia, even read the alphabet. While preparing for this trip, I had met the new head of the Yugoslav National Tourist Office in London. He was called Ante, and his English wasn't terribly good, but his enthusiasm infectious. He had an assistant called Branka who became a good friend and who also gave me the name of a contact in Sarajevo. This was Sveto, short for Svetozar, who turned out to be the head of English at Sarajevo University. His English was impeccable, he was an honorary member of one of the Oxford colleges, and he translated books from Serbo-Croat to English. Later I befriended the whole family, and Sveto and his wife visited me in England.

Yugoslavia intrigued me greatly and as it was not covered in *The Young Traveller* series, I proposed that it should be and was commissioned to write it. This meant many more journeys and a great deal of reading about its complex culture and history. Ante, my enthusiastic contact at the Yugoslav National Tourist Office, was only too glad to arrange further journeys and the necessary introductions to those who could help me on all aspect of Yugoslav life.

With so much material, I looked around for places where I could make good use of it. Yugoslavia's beautiful and varied countryside, magnificent coastline, low-ish prices and sense of independence from the Communist bloc has made it an increasingly popular holiday destination, and I learned that the publishers, Jonathan Cape, were starting a *Travellers' Guide* series to up-and-coming destinations. Not only that, but a subsidiary of Jonathan cape called Jackdaw Publications were publishing a series of educational titles dealing with various historical subjects focussing on facsimiles of relevant documents. At my suggestion they agreed to include the assassination of the Archduke Franz Ferdinand in Sarajevo in 1914, triggering the First World War.

The assassin was Gavrilo Princip, an 18-year-old Serb student whose footprints were sunk into the pavement at the point where he stood when he fired the fatal shot. These footprints were destroyed following Yugoslavia's civil war, but the sight of them had intrigued me, as had the documents in the adjacent museum. They also held a certain irony, for they were on a street corner where the Archduke's chauffeur had hesitated, unsure of which way to go and thus giving Gavrilo time to take aim. Sveto was immensely helpful in guiding me towards other documents, one of which was a record in French of the trial of Gavrilo Princip who could not be given a death sentence due to his age, but who was sent to prison, where he died of tuberculosis.

Sarajevo, which had not impressed me on first sight, now struck me as a thoroughly fascinating city, no doubt assisted by Sveto's knowledge of it. He even offered to introduce me to an old man who had been part of the assassination conspiracy but, alas, age had completely obliterated his memory.

And then, quite suddenly, Gordon Cooper who had brought Yugoslavia into my life died of a heart attack. He was in South Africa at the time. Fortuitously I was at his flat going through his mail when the phone call came through. It was a big shock, and for a moment I couldn't think what to do, but then decided it was probably best to get on to his bank. They were a little cautious in their reaction to the voice of a strange woman, but I managed to convince them I was no more than a messenger, and in due course the bank got in touch with solicitors and things went ahead according to legal requirements.

Following Gordon's death, I had to come clean with the *Sphere* that in fact I had been writing some of the articles for him. They gave me a test article to do then took me on, and it was good to have a regular, if small, income. From this I built up, writing regularly for a publication called *Medical News*, quite often for *The Lady,* the *Scotsman,* and the travel trade press.

I continued to visit Finland regularly throughout the 1960s, sometimes coinciding with the school summer holidays when I would join Annikki on her island. This was off the south-west coast of Finland and reached by rowing boat. I loved staying there. By now I'd done quite a lot of camping with George and this had given me a greater appreciation that a little basic living and discomfort could amply be compensated for by a new understanding of the natural surroundings in which one was experiencing them. It was also during this period that I did some editing for the Finnish Foreign Office.

Eastern Europe began to feature regularly in our travel plans, partly due to George who was lecturing on the subject and partly because of an unexpected spin-off. I then belonged to a professional group of travel writers and was approached by one of its members, Richard Moore, who turned out to be the London Editor of the long-established American Fodor Guide book series. He was looking for someone to do the annual revision of their titles on several East European countries. Would I be interested? A regular commission that was well paid? - wouldn't I just!

In addition to Yugoslavia, I paid my first visits to Bulgaria, Czechoslovakia, Hungary, and Romania which had all become part of what became known as the Warsaw Pact countries under Russia's influence. The fact was that the post-World War Two plan that Europe's eastern countries should democratically choose their future forms of government never truly came to happen. One by one they fell under communist influence, backed by the Soviet Union, and though one by one they protested in one form or another (Hungary in 1956, Czechoslovakia in 1968 as George was to witness) it was only in the last decade of the 20th century that they finally became truly independent.

In the wider world, the 1960s saw the end of colonialism in much of Africa: Tanzania in 1961, Kenya in 1963, the Rhodesias (Zambia/Zimbabwe) in 1964/65. In 1963, President Kennedy was assassinated in Dallas, Texas, and in1965 Winston Church died. Other major happenings were at a more personal level. Dad died in January 1966, Nick and Claire went to University, and my drinking substantially increased. Dad's death was unexpected. He was riddled with rheumatoid arthritis, though he had found a new lease of life when he acquired an electric car which gave him the freedom to drive to the shop, though I took over his old Ford and still drove him to the shop when he did not feel like driving himself. His death began with a chesty cough which rapidly worsened. He was admitted to hospital and died in the early hours of next morning with what was diagnosed as viral pneumonia. It was the first time I had experienced a really close and sudden death.

Len came over immediately to help me sort out the paper work. We visited the Chapel of Rest and it was good to see Dad looking so peaceful. Sinette came soon after, once she had arranged for the in-laws to look after the children. Marcel arrived to represent the Swiss family, and a Vicar friend took the funeral service. It all went smoothly in a numb sort of way.

As for the drinking, I didn't really notice it happening until much later, in retrospect. We still did not have it in the house other than, exceptionally, to launch *The Young Traveller in Finland*, which was followed a few years later by *The Young Traveller in Yugoslavia.* But I was travelling more and more and made good use of the cheaper drinks abroad, especially wine and, in Yugoslavia, the cheap and very potent *slivovica*. I really didn't understand what Dad had against it; maybe it would have helped if we could have discussed it.

Once the funeral was over and Dad's straightforward will sorted out, Sinette and Len came to have a Serious Talk. It was mainly about the best decision to make with regard to Mum. I'd already given it some thought because I knew better than anyone how poorly Mum could be in the middle of night if she got an attack of hypoglycaemia; then the quickest remedy was to give her a sweetened drink, but it really was not sensible to leave her alone overnight, let alone over several nights. My first tentative thought was that it might make sense to move to Cambridge, somewhere near Sinette and Len who would be on hand in case of a crisis when I was away. And she would love being near the grandchildren.

When I told Sinette and Len, the former was astounded. "I never thought we'd persuade you to leave London!"

Well, I wasn't that wedded to London, but I did need to be within reasonably easy reach of it and the public transport links with Cambridge had improved a great deal over the years. Sinette immediately set about looking for a suitable small house in the Girton area where they lived and was not long in coming up with one. It was modern, with two-bedrooms, semi-detached and about a mile from them. We put our bungalow on the market. Everything happened pretty quickly, and in April that year I was driving in the wake of the removals van with Mum and a loudly protesting Sappho. A mongrel she may have been, but from her distinctive voice, there was undoubtedly a fair percentage of Persian in her.

In the meantime, George came to stay whenever his lecture tours brought him in our direction. East Anglia wasn't quite as convenient as London but he seemed happy to adapt. Sappho, who preferred men, usually curled up on his sleeping bag. Of the two bedrooms I was allocated the larger one, which served as my office and 'publishing house' as Mum rather grandly called it. And it's true that by then I had three books to my name as well as contacts for regular contributions to a tidy list of good publications.

Out in the wider world, changes were happening, in particular in the Eastern Bloc where the straightjacket effect of the Cominform had been overturned in Czechoslovakia by the rise of Alexander Dubček. This Slovak politician eventually became Czechoslovakia's leader in January 1967 when he ruled over what became known as the

'Prague Spring'. I was fortunate enough to visit the country during that period, and there was a tangible sense of optimism. It was on that trip that I befriended a Czech engineer; I knew him by his nickname Franta and we remained friends for some decades.

It took a while to get used to the semi-rural atmosphere of the outskirts of Cambridge, but I was travelling quite a lot, frequently in London, and life was busy. When in London, I stayed with Philippa who, despite the age gap, was now a valued close friend. By now I had graduated from Dad's old Ford, via a van to a Morris Minor that I bought from Len's father Joe, now a widower who had also joined us in Girton.

The relationship with George had changed subtly. He no longer hid the fact that he wanted us to make our lives together. Even though in my late thirties, I still wasn't sure I wanted to give up my independence but anyway there was no question of it since he was as married as ever and had always made it clear, that even if I agree to it, he would not divorce until all three sons were independent adults. The youngest, Nick, was planning an academic career but had yet to go through university. But I did understand better the unsatisfactory basis on which his marriage was founded.

He and Marjorie had met in a Cambridge bookshop a few weeks before he was shot down. They had gone out together and got on well, but George was reluctant to have a formal relationship given the dangerous times. Then he was shot down. Marjorie corresponded with him while he was a p.o.w. and when he finally returned home in 1945, he found she had become very friendly with his parents. Rightly or wrongly he felt that it was expected they should get married and he did not have a clear enough idea of what he wanted for his future to put up any obstacles. The only thing he was sure about was his desire to return to climbing.

I also became familiar with something called the YRC which stood for the Yorkshire Ramblers' Club - a misnomer if ever there were one, for this group of serious climbers and cavers did everything but ramble. In fact, they had led some major climbing and caving expeditions in quite remote parts of the world. George's involvement with the YRC and its members did nothing to improve his commitment as a husband and father.

Increasingly he was away on mountains or expeditions. Though it did not make for an ideal marriage or fatherhood, it did quite soon provide him with an opportunity for increasing his income.

Following demobilisation, George had done a rapid teacher training course, and soon found regular employment as a geography teacher, at first in the Lake District and later in his home county of Yorkshire. In the 1950s he was offered the opportunity to join a survey expedition to the Antarctic island of South Georgia whose members were privileged each to have a feature of the landscape named after them, thus adding the Spenceley Glacier to the world map.

On this expedition he was joined by two men who were to become friends for life. He also experienced an adventure that triggered an insatiable appetite for more, decided to turn this into a talk for public consumption, and discovered that he was rather good at this new profession. He was adopted by a leading lecture agency and continued to give talks to societies, libraries, luncheon clubs and public schools round the country for most of the rest of his life. We still met quite frequently but I think he came to accept that a permanent relationship was not on any imminent agenda and we continued our separate travels - mine always rather short and hurried and under the auspices of this or that tourist organisation, and George at more leisure, usually in preparation of another talk, and sometimes not alone.

In the meantime the world continued to become an increasingly troubled place, particularly in the Middle East, and especially in Palestine. With the rising persecution of the Jews between the two World Wars, their numbers migrating to the British Mandate of Palestine increased to the point that restrictions were imposed in 1939 hardly, with hindsight, the best of timing. Following the Holocaust it was inevitable that the numbers soared giving rise to bloody conflict between Jews, Arabs and British and equally the rise of a Jewish resistance. One of its major results was the Six-Day War of June 1967. This resulted in Israeil gain of the West Bank from Jordan, the Gaza Strip and Sinai Peninsula from Egypt, and the Goran Heights from Syria whose after-effects rumbled on for decades. With the great benefit of hindsight, there is a certain irony in the fact that 1967 also turned out to be the Summer of Love; then hundreds of thousands, if not more, met to celebrate new moral freedoms and experiment increasingly with drugs, legacies which have left their mark well into the 21st century, the fiftieth anniversary of that summer being celebrated in 2017..

However, other troubles were happening nearer home. In 1968, George left for several weeks in Romania with a young

Australian. He had been attracted to it when passing through it on an earlier return journey from Turkey and now wanted to investigate it further. That was the summer I went twice to Italy and on the second occasion fell a little in love again, this time with a BBC producer called Harry. Married of course. I'm not sure how I ever justified relationships with married men in my mind; probably I didn't try on the principle that no marriage was going to be broken on my account. But we both acted like teenagers, though neither of us was far off forty.

This time George's trip to Romania was to have memorable moments of a quite different nature. Indeed I'd been aware of them, without associating them with him. They had taken place overnight in the month before my trip to Florence. As usual I had switched on the Radio Four morning programme when I woke up and to my horror heard that Czechoslovakia had been invaded by the Warsaw Pact countries in retaliation for the Prague Spring.

George, it turned out, had been camping near Prague Airport on his way back from Romania. I forget what had happened to the Australian lass, but he had been awakened by the sound of a considerable numbers of planes landing at the airport and found himself in the middle of the invasion. His photographs were impressive, especially those of young Czechs clambering over Russian tanks and daubing them with swastikas and the words *'Go Home!'* The young Russians and, especially, those from allied countries were completely bewildered as they had been led to believe that they would be welcomed as liberators. George spent the day handing out freedom leaflets in Prague and explaining with profound regret why he could not fill his car with Czechs wanting to leave the country; but he did take out many letters to post and promised to 'tell the world' of the truth - though he had no great hope that the world would do much about it.

I have to admit that his dramas were a good deal more interesting than mine. He had been interviewed by newspapers and radio, and of course it would make a fascinating contribution to his new lecture. In due course I heard that my Czech friend had been out of the country on business at the time of the invasion but had been transported back by the Red Cross. But I felt sad for my Czech friends who had been so enjoying the freedoms of the Prague Spring.

My relationship with the BBC producer ran its course. I remember it being extremely painful because in those days, at least in

61

my experience, married men disposed towards such relationships indulged in the wishful thinking that after a while it was OK to modify quite intense feelings to those of a good friendship, usually without mentioning the fact to the partner concerned. It was a hard way to learn that being 'the other woman' entitled you to nothing more but intense feelings and, ultimately, a profound sense of loss. At the time I was too busy feeling sorry for myself to register, in 1969, the first landing of a man on the moon by the US in Apollo 8. I told George about Harry, but I don't think it made much impression, except for the one positive outcome: that I ended up by doing quite a few Radio Four documentary programmes.

The move brought one more interesting outcome. I had never lost the hope that one day I might learn to fly, so on an impulse one day I went to Marshall Airport on the outskirts of Cambridge, found it had a gliding club and joined it. I loved gliding, though I never went solo, and eventually gave up because I couldn't afford it; but in the course of quite a few lessons I had that amazing experience of hanging in the air looking out over the flat East Anglian landscape, especially in the autumn when at that time they had the custom of burning the stubble fields. I somehow managed to persuade Harry that it would be a good idea to do a programme on gliding.

As already mentioned, I had become involved with the American series Fodor Guides editing several of their titles, notably in Scandinavia and Eastern Europe. It was a good regular annual income and provided an excellent reason to re-visit my favourite countries. And it was particularly fortuitous because several of the countries were also among George's lecture subjects so that we could both justify spending time there in the interests of our professional work.

Towards the end of the 1960s, I had a major boost to my professional standing. A travel-writing friend who was about to join a major national newspaper was looking for someone she might recommend to replace her as a regular contributor to another newspaper. She asked me if I might be interested, and of course I was. I was given a test run, and accepted, and so I joined the regular freelance team of *The Financial Times*. Initially there were three of us covering travel subjects in the Saturday edition of the paper; we'd meet up regularly with the Deputy Editor to put forward our ideas and establish a timetable for them. In due course, one of us died and the remaining two continued until a staff travel correspondent was appointed. But I had fourteen years of regular writing for them and it opened many doors.

Nevertheless, with the benefit of hindsight, there was also one major blot on the 1960s, though of course I did not recognise it at the time. That was my growing dependence on alcohol.

1970-79: courage to change

It was insidious. Initially, my main awareness was how much easier it was to get on with putting words on a blank sheet of paper after a couple of glasses of wine. To that extent I had become cautious about my use of this new 'friend' and switched from my favoured tipple whisky to sherry and eventually wine. What I did not notice - or allow myself to recognise - was that it never stayed at two glasses; after a certain point, I would feel sleepy, would have a doze and then somehow my mind didn't seem quite as lively any more, unless I went out for another bottle. And that was another odd thing. I never seemed to have quite enough.

I began to hide bottles, though from whom I could not have said. The only regular visitor I had was Jean from just down the road whose husband had multiple sclerosis. Mum had taken to visiting him regularly when his wife Jean was out at work, and I took on the same role, especially because he was interested in writing. Jean would sometimes call in and I certainly did not want her seeing an open bottle in the kitchen, so I kept it in the pantry or, if I were working upstairs, in my wardrobe. Looking back it is so easy to see that paranoia was setting in, but at the time such precautions seemed quite normal.

As Mum's health continued to deteriorate, she spent an increasing amount of time at Sinette's, notably if I were away for more than a night or two. By then quite a lot of my travelling was solo for, with the *F.T.* (as I came to call the *Financial Times)* as one of my 'regulars', there was no problem in getting assistance in travel or accommodation. The main disadvantage was that it tended to be a rather brief and breathless form of travel. Fortunately, *F.T.* readers adapted to learning about the sort of places they might not have considered in the past.

Whether it was to do with my drinking or my advancing years, I was aware of beginning to feel restless. Another incident may have added to this when I learned of the sudden death of my dear Finnish friend Annikki Setälä. It was also becoming clear that the days when Mum could be left alone were numbered. She had one or two falls and was 'rescued' by neighbours. Sinette and Len decided that their plans to build a small annexe on to their house had better be brought forward and, with Sinette's usual energy, they set about making it a reality sooner rather than later.

I was split. I knew Mum would probably feel lonelier in her new surroundings for Sinette and family led busy lives and Nick and Claire were in their teens with their own preoccupations. Nick's late teens were particularly chequered, including quite a lot of travel. In due course he went to Bristol to study philosophy and Claire to Warwick to study education/psychology. On the other hand it was a bit late for me to try and embark on a new career and anyway I'd worked hard to make progress in this one.

The annexe to the Shields' home materialised at speed. It was self-contained and compact with a small living room, a smaller bedroom and its own shower. The annexe was reached from the Shields' dining room in which Mum would share her meals with the family and, though I was a little concerned that she might feel a bit isolated for much of the day, it clearly made sense that she would never again be alone at night. So Mum and Sappho moved across to live with my sister and family.

Sappho soon became a problem, disappearing for longer and longer periods. Sinette would stand behind the door calling her in a fair imitation of Mum's accent and the cat would eventually sneak in to find the door slammed behind her. But this really couldn't go on indefinitely. It was decided that we must find another home for her and this we did, surprisingly easily. She was a pretty cat, quite small for her six years and a middle aged couple fell for her instantly. I let them take her, basket, cat food, bag and baggage and all, on their first visit before I could change my mind. Then I went out and bought a bottle of whisky. It was agreed that I would telephone once after a few days to make sure she had settled in. I did and she had, and that was the last I heard of her.

Out in the wide world, the Vietnam War dragged on inflicting terrible casualties, perhaps best remembered by many of us for that iconic photograph of a naked child running towards the cameras, her whole being expressing agony and fear. It was one of many photographs that contributed to growing opposition to the war in the West, and especially in the United States where massive student protests in particular led to a number of student deaths dividing the nation even further. Richard Nixon was now in power and began the gradual removal of its ground forces. Direct US military involvement ended in August 1973, and the two halves of the country re-united in 1976. It was earlier in 1973 that the U.K. finally joined the European Economic Community and two years later that we held our first ever national referendum in order to stay 'in Europe'.

Now that there was no anxiety about leaving Mum alone, I looked for a job in Cambridge, increasingly anxious that, for whatever reason, I should establish my independence. I was also aware that running even a small house on my own needed perhaps a rather more secure source of income than was guaranteed by my writing. In the end I found employment three days a week editing some of a series of international biographic encyclopaedias, each focusing on a particular profession - e.g. education, management, medicine, research. Looking back it was in a way the textual equivalent of the photographic 'selfies' that were to follow some decades later. Anyway, it paid tolerably well, and as importantly, I got into the habit of working late and making sure I had a bottle of wine available when I was alone.

George started to worry about my drinking. "Just don't drink on your own," he said, putting on his pleading spaniel look. His insistence began to annoy me. The fact was that my depressive tendencies had returned with a vengeance; the drink helped to deaden them, but I didn't or wouldn't recognise that alcohol probably also contributed to the depression or that it took increasingly more to have effect. George took to asking me when he telephoned whether I was drinking, and I took to devising a system whereby I could truthfully answer that I was not. This involved going out to buy a bottle of wine (invariably I ran out mid-afternoon) before George's daily phone call. If for some reason this was later than expected, I'd rush out and back again hoping he would not ring while I was out. In retrospect, it seems so childish now going to such extremes, but the deviousness of the addict I was to discover had few boundaries.

Mum quite often came to spend the week-end with me. If she noticed anything amiss she did not make any comment; anyway at that time I still had a degree of control for limited periods. She also still went to Switzerland once a year. By now we were making arrangements for her to be taken to the aircraft by wheelchair and, of course, there was always someone to meet her at the other end. In the summer of 1974 she wrote to tell us she would be staying a little

66

longer as there had been some complications with her thyroid which she'd had removed some years earlier when a growth had appeared. In the end I decided to go over and bring her back with me.

I was shocked when I saw her, and her voice was very rough and odd. With time it became rougher and odder, and finally she was diagnosed with cancer of the larynx. Sinette and I didn't worry too much at first since she had already had a cancerous growth successfully removed years earlier; but it was clear that she was generally very unwell. Initially we put this down to the radio therapy treatment she was having.

Finally I made an appointment to see her consultant. He was kind but grave. He said that the cancer had spread to other parts of her body and that at her age and in her condition it was not realistic to expect a cure. The best they could do was to keep her out of pain and as comfortable as possible. She had a small room to herself in Addenbrookes Hospital in Cambridge and we could visit more or less when we wanted. In the meantime, deadlines still had to be met, the house and garden kept in order and meals prepared. I loathed gardening - the previous owners had bequeathed us a lot of rose bushes whose main purpose in life seemed to be to tear at my skin or inflict me with plagues of white-, green- or black-fly. Though I probably didn't appreciate it at the time, Sinette was a brick and did most of the gardening for me. My cooking was modest in the extreme. Perhaps the only real credit I can chalk up for myself is that for the last week or two of Mum's life I stopped drinking. And in a weird way I enjoyed my visits. She and I had always been good at mutual silence. Sometimes I held her hand. When I left she always said, "*Courage, chérie.*" I envied her lack of fear.

And still in the end I let her down. Among the things that cropped up at that time was a trip to Jamaica which had been agreed some time earlier. For this I needed a number of vaccinations, including one that needed updating. Probably because I was not in a very good state of health, I reacted rather badly to one of these, ran a temperature and felt quite ill. Reluctantly I decided it would be foolish to visit the hospital and Sinette agreed to go instead. Mum, alas, died in the early hours of the next morning. It was Len who rang to tell me as Sinette was too upset. We spent most of the day together, while we listed and dealt with as many of the formalities as possible. To our relief, the priest who had been vicar of the church we attended when living in London's suburbs agreed to take the service, and we arranged for a rose bush to be planted in the gardens of the crematorium in Mum's memory. My sobriety lasted until just after the funeral.

My memories of those days and the weeks that followed are very muddled. The trip to Jamaica was at least a distraction from the loss of someone who, until then, had been my most constant companion. Deadlines and the rest of the business of living took up every other available moment. All the same I was aware of an underlying unease and dissatisfaction that lay beyond the grief of bereavement. Eventually I traced it, perhaps in one of my less sober moments, to a resentment that my life had been on 'hold' for a very long time due to George's circumstances. I wasn't even sure that I wanted to spend the rest of my days with him or indeed anyone. In fact, I wasn't sure of anything except that I wanted change.

I found myself recalling a project I'd had many years earlier: one of those 'I-wonder-what-would-happen-if...' fantasies whereby I'd get on a bus or drive to .... anywhere, rent a room and see what happened. With our parents gone, Sinette happily settled with husband, two children, and me with no finally agreed ties with anyone else, this could be the opportunity to find out. After all, in my early forties I couldn't afford to hang around forever. Perhaps a sensible first step would be to sell the house and move into a flat in the town centre where I could take part in things and rejoin the human race.

I must have mentioned it to George for his expression of unutterable dismay was, followed by the more familiar spaniel look. "No, no, please don't do that." He had long insisted that circumstances would change and then we would be able to plan as we wished. I wasn't clear as to what the circumstances were except that it was something to do with money. But I agreed not to make any major hasty decisions. I did, however, make one for the more immediate future, and that was to spend Christmas with my friend Sally, in whose parents' pub in East Anglia I had learned to drink, but who had now bought a house with a friend and lived in Cornwall. From there I planned to join George for New Year in the Lake District. It did not occur to me that it would also be Sinette's first Christmas without Mum and she might have liked to have another member of the family around. Addiction makes you very self-centred.

We drank too much over Christmas - I think even Sally was startled by my intake - and I had a hair-raising drive to the Lakes. It was still relatively early in the history of motorways and I was far from experienced in the use of them. That New Year left no particular memories but I remember assuring George that if I continued with what he called my 'solo drinking' I would do something about it. What I would do was less clear. I had heard of an organisation that specialised in Recovery, and imagined it to be something to do with people in grubby raincoats swigging straight from a bottle and sleeping on park benches. Of course the inevitable happened, ironically with Sally's brother Harry who was now married to his Janet and called in on the way to visiting his mother. He was clearly taken aback by my consumption but accepted my assurance that I was all right, and I suspect he was relieved to leave me to it.

The next morning I felt terrible but something more persistent than excuse and justification led me to remember the promise to George. I reached for the telephone directory. There was nothing listed under the Recovery people except the name and telephone number of one or two members purporting to provide information. I took a swig from the dregs of a bottle of Martini and rang one of them.

A pleasant male voice interrupted the ringing tone, I think he said his name was Brian, and could he help. I said I wanted information about his organisation, told him my first name and to my surprise he launched into a story about himself. I began to feel quite sorry for him. It seemed he'd had a terrible time; I think lost jobs, a broken marriage and police cells came into it.

Eventually he stopped and said, "So you see, the Fellowship has given me back my life."

Then he asked, "And how about you Sylvie? Are you on the programme? You sound as though you are."

He'd been so nice and clearly wanted me to be on the programme - whatever it was - so I said I was in order not to disappoint him, though I had no idea what it meant. I added that I wanted to know when there might be a meeting in Cambridge. There was a pause while he looked it up, then he told me there was one in a couple of days time, adding, "Unfortunately I can't go for the next couple of weeks, but I can arrange for someone to meet you." It seemed there was a sister organisation whose members were relatives of alcoholics. I assured him I could find my own way to the meeting, though when the time came I nearly had second thoughts.

Fortunately I didn't and two days later, I parked the car and made my way to a building that announced itself as a day centre for senior citizens. The front entrance led into a hallway from which it was clear from the volume of conversation that I had arrived at my first Recovery meeting.

A middle-aged lady in an artist's smock noticed me first. "I'm Joyce," she stated. "Is this your first meeting?" I admitted that it was and that my name was Sylvie. "Ah," Joyce said. "Well, don't worry about anything. Pete is doing the chair tonight - he's great. You don't have to say a thing if you don't want to. Hang on a bit and I'll get you some stuff."

'Stuff' turned out to be some leaflets and a list of local meetings of which there did not seem to be many. Joyce explained "We start the meeting with a few announcements, then Pete talks about his story - how he came to be here, what life is like now, and then we go round the room for anyone to share if they want to. But don't worry," she repeated. "You don't have to say a thing if you don't want to."

Soon after, people started sitting down. Joyce patted a seat next to her for me to sit on. Someone read a short announcement stating that the group was not connected with any other organisation and was totally self-supporting through its own contributions, and that the only requirement for membership was a desire to stop drinking. Did I have such a desire? But this was not the time for head conversations and I settled back in my chair as Pete, fortyish, dark haired, relaxed, said "My name is Pete and I'm an alcoholic."

There followed a story that was truly more fascinating than most radio dramas. Pete had travelled the world, half the time not appearing to remember where he was going, been through two marriages, ended up in police cells, woken up in hospital several times, the last time to find a stranger sitting by his bed announcing that he was a member of a Recovery group and did Pete want to stop drinking?

"And to my astonishment," Pete said, "I heard myself say that I did".

But did I, I asked myself again? And could it be that simple? Apparently not. Pete had skidded in and out of Recovery for a year, but once the seed had been sown and there was visible proof at every meeting of how sobriety worked, it became more attractive than the alternative.

When he had finished, Pete asked if anyone else wanted to share. After a couple of people had commented, it went silent and so they went round the room. When it came to me I said, "My name is Sylvie and I ... I think I may be an alcoholic."

"Well done," Joyce murmured beside me.

What on earth had I started, I wondered.

As I left, Joyce thrust a piece of paper at me with her telephone number on it. Well, I didn't have to ring it, did I?

----oOo----

George was delighted when I told him what I'd done. Ironically we went to celebrate. I elected to drink ginger ale, and very soon learned my first lesson. George soon got into the habit of ordering his wine and my ginger ale without further consultation. I found resentment smouldering and consulted Joyce who gave me the answer. It sounded - probably was - childish, but it worked.

"I'd prefer it," I told George, "if you asked me what I want to drink and not assume you know. After all, it's my decision."

He looked puzzled but proceeded to do so. Resentment became tempered by amusement. Clever those folk. Unfortunately I didn't register all that they said. Although I didn't find our pub visits particularly enjoyable, it was good to be able to go out together and I slowly realised that I had managed two, three, then four weeks without touching alcohol. This brought its own problems. If I hadn't had a drink for four weeks, how could I possibly be an alcoholic? The niggling resentment returned. Again I consulted Joyce.

"It's quite simple," she said. "If you think you have got over the problem, why don't you set out to have a couple of drinks in the evening and stick to that?" And even as she said it, I knew there was no way I could.

George was in the middle of a busy lecture season and away quite a lot. That summer his great friend Tom also introduced him to a new form of adventuring: canoeing. This was on Lake Windermere and George was so taken by it that he agreed to go on a long distance canoe venture in Canada with Tom the following year. He also thought I should be introduced to it too, so we bought an 18 ft. aluminium Grumman canoe and joined a canoeing association with whom we went on camping week-ends paddling down the upper Thames. In addition to my regular writing commitments I'd decided to have a go at a book on Iceland as there seemed to be a gap in the market.

Still pleased at my success without alcohol, I planned my days round my writing, occasional Recovery meetings, visits to London where I continued to spend a night or two with Philippa once or twice a week, and running the house. Occasionally I would allow myself a glass of wine and the heavens did not fall in, but the trouble was that opened bottles of wine demanded to be drunk. It had to be acknowledged in due course that I was trying to control my drinking rather than to stop it. At meetings I heard references to the Twelve Steps to recovery, to getting 'a sponsor', to having 'a God of your understanding', but did not really consider them to apply to me. The other comment I did not register was: *if you don't take a drink you can't get drunk.*

Sometimes it's difficult to cope with simplicity.

So I dickered on for eighteen months, drinking much less but learning as I went along how progressive this condition is, so that much less continued to make me ever more ill, and not least ever more anxious. The fact that I was still drinking, even though it was considerably less, began increasingly to trouble my conscience, so I stopped going to meetings.

And then one evening George rang and said, "Forget that buying-a-flat-in-Cambridge idea. Something's happened. I'll be down early this week-end." He had recently returned from West Africa and I knew had found his father in a very poor condition. Since George's mother had died 'Pop,' as his father was known, had taken on one housekeeper and married another. I thought I could guess what might have happened.

I was right. Pop had died peacefully in his sleep at the good age of ninety-four. His will catered mainly for the rest of the family. George felt he could now look to his own future.

There were long discussions about where we should live. I remained obstinate about staying in the southern half of the country. Mid-forties was too late to move north into Spenceley-Yorkshire territory, and I did still need to be within reasonable access of London offices and airport. We finally settled - almost by putting a pin in the map - on north Oxfordshire, which was centrally placed for George's lecture tours and certainly as convenient for London as Cambridge had been. At the time we both overlooked his canoeing plans in Canada with Tom.

The move was further complicated by George picking up a mystery bug in West Africa. He was quite ill and in an isolation ward for a while, but we found an affordable house in the village of Steeple Aston, between Oxford and Banbury, and planned to move in April 1976.

While he recovered from his West African bug, I sold the house in Girton, moved in with Len's father who was now living in the street next to Sinette and Len, arranged for gas, electricity, telephones, etc. in Steeple Aston; and organised removals men.

Just across the valley from Steeple Aston was Upper Heyford and its airbase leased to the Americans. Quite a few of them lived in the village including our immediate neighbours, Bill and Louise, who came over with a tray of tea almost as soon as we arrived.

Clearly, once George and I were sharing a home my increasingly erratic controlled drinking would not go unnoticed so I decided to return to the Recovery meetings. I checked the local meetings and found there were then two in Oxford and one in Banbury. Oxford, I thought, sounded more intellectual so early on I found my way to its Monday evening meeting. It was rather big and I didn't say very much. Afterwards a woman a little younger than me rushed out after me as I went to the car and gave me her telephone number.

It was about this time that my favourite Swiss aunt Agnes died, and soon after another aunt by marriage. Without fully appreciating it at the time, I had reached that age when the older generation vanishes with startling rapidity. We were informed that I'd inherited certain items, including a painting and small pieces of furniture. Eric, one of George's oldest climbing friends, suggested that we should take his camping car and go and collect them. Alas, I also found I had inherited a crate of wine. It was an awful journey as George and Eric drank their way back across France (not 'my' wine - they bought their own, but still) and I thought I'd go mad. It was far too early days for me to understand that non-alcoholics (whom we often referred to as 'civilians') were incapable of understanding that 'staying stopped' was by far the most difficult part of sobriety, nor how stupid they sounded after a few drinks.

With so much going on, we overlooked George's pre-arranged trip to Canada with Tom for the summer of 1976. The two men's plans had consolidated and they were now aiming at following in the canoe strokes of a British trio who had perished in the Barren Lands of Canada some forty years earlier. And now the trip was fast approaching.

Soon after our return from Switzerland, Tom came to spend the week-end with us and discuss plans for their journey. He had been with George in South Georgia, had travelled the world on other expeditions and proved to be an indefatigable open-air person. During his travels Tom had come upon a story that attracted him like greatly. It was a tale of British travellers who had attempted to winter in one of the remotest parts of Canada, known as the Barren Grounds presumably because they were just that. But long distance canoeing in Canada, just the two of them?

When I first heard of it I repeated in disbelief, "*Canoe? Canada?*"

"Just imagine sitting there and being carried along by the current!" Tom said.

"And what happens when you're paddling against a howling gale?"

"Ah well, it won't be roses *all* the way."

"OK, tell me about these Brits then."

Apparently it started with a guy called David Hanbury, now an almost forgotten English explorer, who arrived on the Canadian scene in the late 19th century. During a series of remarkable journeys, mostly with Inuit companions, he was the first to canoe the Thelon and Hanbury river which now bears his name. Sometime later, in 1904, Tom explained, a fellow called John Hornby followed in Hanbury's footsteps and became equally obsessed with the Barren Grounds. Then in the summer of 1926, he appeared on Great Slave Lake with two unlikely companions: one Harold Adlard, an ex-RAF pilot, and the other his second cousin, Edgar Christian, an 18-year-old schoolboy from Dover College. With these two novices he proposed to do what not even the boldest trapper would consider: to winter on the Thelon. They left Fort Reliance in late July; they were never seen alive again.

"But *why*?" I persisted. "Why would you want to do something so dangerous?"

"Why has anyone wanted to do anything for the first time?" Tom countered. "It's what man - and increasingly woman - has done since the beginning of time: pushed out the boundaries, gone round the next corner, climbed the next mountain."

I scowled. "Well, I don't like the sound of it a bit. I'm not marrying George so that he can drown himself five minutes later."

"More like three months than five minutes. Anyway neither Tom nor I have any intention of drowning. The British didn't drown either; they tried to overwinter and died of starvation."

"The trouble in their case," Tom went on, "was that the lifeblood of the Barren Grounds is caribou - what we call reindeer.

The herds flow like a great tide back and forth, from timber to tundra. But they are fickle; it's a rhythmic flow, but unpredictable. The caribou may pass the same spot in the same month for a dozen years running and the next year not come at all. For good reason it is often called the land of feast or famine. And for the three men who built their cabin on the banks of the Thelon, it turned out to be a land of famine."

They had found a little meat and fish, he said, but the caribou migration on which they depended had passed them by. A Royal Canadian Mounted Police patrol found their bodies two years later, two rolled in blankets outside, one on his bunk within the cabin,. The details of that tragic winter would only have been surmised, their deaths quickly forgotten, but for the courageous persistence of the schoolboy Edgar Christian. From October onwards, he kept a daily diary, a remarkable record without trace of fear or self pity, showing only concern for his companions. We learn that John Hornby died, exhausted by his efforts to find food, in April., and a few weeks later Adlard died too. Somehow, for another month, alone and with no hope, Edgar Christian remained alive, keeping the diary, recording in meticulous detail an account of each day's search for food. This diary, which was later published, was now housed in the library of Dover College.

I found myself trying to imagine waking in that freezing loneliness to face yet another day with a couple of corpses as company. And couldn't.

But it was a great relief to know that Tom had a very healthy respect for remote rivers - a good deal more respect it seemed to me than my new housemate. I was not looking forward to the summer - ostensibly our first complete summer together, but which I would spend alone in a new house in an area where I knew no one except a few members of a Fellowship to which I was not at all sure I really belonged.

Indeed, Tom's week-end with us proved to be especially significant in another way, for it marked my return to that Fellowship. Following our return from Switzerland with the crate of wine, I had really struggled. A major part of the problem was that I was seriously doubtful whether I qualified as an alcoholic. If you had a drink after joining Recovery it was called a 'slip'. I decided to use one of my twelve inherited bottles to have an 'experiment', and George decided it was probably better to do it in his company than on my own. So we opened a bottle. The skies did not fall in. I didn't particularly enjoy it, but all that happened was my head felt very muddled..

We had a foreign visitor the next evening, so I continued the experiment, this time adding a pre-dinner sherry to it. Our friend left fairly early, I didn't feel very well but certainly it was nothing resembling a hangover. It was simply that my brain felt completely scrambled as though it wouldn't function properly. Alone in the house while George and Tom canoed a section of the Oxford Canal, I rang one or two members of the Fellowship. They didn't sound surprised. *Get to a meeting* was the universal advice, and suggested one that evening at a local rehab centre. I switched on the radio and couldn't seem to make sense of anything. I decided to go the following evening, after Tom had left. And tried not to notice that the muddled feeling was getting worse with an added element of fear.

Later that day I went to collect Tom and George and the canoe. Tom left soon after, and George took me to the meeting, a bit puzzled as to what all the fuss was about. The main thing I took in that evening was a short lecture from an old-timer who had been a member of the Fellowship forever. He pointed out that stopping drinking was not a problem; staying stopped was. And that every time I'd started again I'd set myself back not so much physically as mentally and spiritually, whatever that meant. And that there was a structured programme for recovery and perhaps it was time I took a look at it.

It was soon after George's departure for Canada that I hit another real low and telephoned a member of one of the Oxford groups who was something to do with TV aerials. He was there in half an hour, persuaded me to eat a raw egg as I had eaten nothing for a couple of days and arranged to take me to the Banbury meeting in a couple of days. Banbury became my home group and, though everything was far from plain sailing forever after, my Recovery career didn't look back.

The year 1976 proved to be the hottest year in memory. Hot bright day followed hot bright day and the grass seed we had sowed on to our untended garden lay dormant. Otherwise we had settled into the village quite well, made friends at the local Red Lion, got to know our neighbours, especially Bill and Louise who were full of admiration for George's project. He had left for Canada some time before Tom with the mission of begging a lift from a seaplane for themselves and the canoe to be transported to the starting point of their river journey. In due course they were deposited on a lake in the middle of nowhere to be greeted by a million mosquitoes.

"*Until that moment,*" George reported in an early letter, "*I think we had forgotten that devastating curse of the North: insect pests. They rose from the lichen at our feet and hung like a malevolent mist around us ; both mosquito and black fly, the latter not merely biting but with each bite taking a lump of us away with them. They flew into our mouths and nostrils, they found their way through the tiniest rift in our clothing, but their favourite place was the ear where they spun and tumbled deep down near the drum.   After a while we were hardly recognisable.*"

On their second day of travel down the Thelon, there was a change in the landscape. Tundra, bare of all but tiny growth, gave way on both sides of the river to sturdy spruce. Here was that strange oasis of the Barrens, an island of comparative fertility, where tundra and tree line merged, the place for which John Hornby and his companions, their British predecessors, headed for his winter quarters fifty years earlier. George and Tom found the remains of the cabin, a rectangle of rough hewn logs set back a little from the river. Small colourful arctic flowers grew in fantastic abundance, contributing to a peaceful and beautiful scene but this was the stage on which was played out the tragedy of that long drawn out winter and delayed spring of 1926-27. Three mounds of earth and stones and the three crude wooden crosses told of the outcome of a human drama in which all the qualities of fortitude, courage, self-sacrifice and devotion were fully displayed. George and Tom walked round the site for a long time in silence.

Back in Oxfordshire I was struggling. Whether or not it was more or less intellectual than Oxford, I found it easier to talk at the Banbury meeting and (perhaps as a result) people found it easier to talk to me. A farmer's wife took me under her wing and, though I probably did not recognise it as such, I used her as a sponsor for a long time, until she died (of cancer, but sober).

And then I had my first working trip abroad in my shaky sobriety. It was to Majorca, then rapidly up and coming, where I was to explore and report on the expanding tourist facilities. I was put up in a splendid hotel and had barely arrived when there was a knock on my door and a waiter appeared with a bottle of wine in a bucket of ice. He put it down with a tray and a glass and bowed himself out. The bottle and I stared at each other. Nobody would know..... Before I could finish the sentence in my head, the old-timer's voice echoed in my head: *it's staying stopped that's the problem.* I rang through to reception and demanded that the bottle be removed and replaced by fruit juice. The girl sounded puzzled. Indeed, the waiter reappeared moments later with a bottle opener. Almost hysterical I got him to understand I wanted the bottle removed and replaced and, mightily surprised, he did as bidden, returning with juice.

Moments later I was gulping the first of very many .... too many.... orange juices. It was probably among the most significant moments of my life.

After that, coincidentally or not, the summer passed OK. I had one more trip: to my dear friends Matti and Ritva in Helsinki. George and I had arranged to meet by the clock in Paddington Station, he from Canada and I from Finland. We made it within two minutes of each other and returned to Steeple Aston to find the grass had grown knee-high....

----oOo---

"Hooray" Sinette yelled down the phone. It was a year later and I had just rung to check that she and Len were free on June 25th and when she asked why told her George and I were planning to marry. *"Marrying at last!"* Claire wrote in our visitors' book, seventeen and cheeky.

It was going to be a small unfussy affair in Banbury's Registry Office, with George's climbing friend Louis, my friend Philippa, Sinette, Len and Claire. Nick had already settled in Australia. I could hear my own voice wobbling as I made the responses during the service. Afterwards we had a splendid meal at the Red Lion, our favourite local. It turned out to be not so difficult to face my wedding without alcohol.

So, I was forty-six, a year sober and newly married. We turned a working trip to Canada into our honeymoon. Both of us tended to be a bit obsessive about travel being 'work'. George was developing a new lecture, mainly based on his canoe venture in The Barrens but he wanted to temper it with more general background on Canada's history and topography. I was always looking for new subjects for the *F.T.* We decided to concentrate on the contrasting worlds of Alberta and the Rockies, and the lowland prairies with their prehistory and broadening economy.

In the meantime George's second son Adrian had made it clear he wanted nothing to do with us except in earlier months when he needed his father's signature in connection with executing his grandfather's will. I decided to have a go at making contact with the youngest, Nick, and spent a lot of time writing what I hoped was a friendly letter. He responded a little stiffly saying he would accept the letter in the spirit in which it was written. He was then at Cambridge University where we went to meet him in due course and also met the young woman, Lorna, who was to become his wife.

Out in the big world, a major event occurred in 1978 with the Camp David Accords signed by Presidents Begin for Israel and Sadat for Egypt, winning them both the Nobel Peace Prize. President Sadat paid for it with his life when he was assassinated the following year by Islamist extremists, and the Accords were to have a rocky ride as reduced conflict gradually gave way to international controversy and renewed bloodshed as an increasing number of Israelis settled on the West Bank

1979-1980: Danube

We'd been married a while when George said, "You know you said you wanted to do a long canoe trip?"

"No. When you came back from Canada with Tom, I remember saying the next time I was coming with you. Though I suppose you could interpret it as the same thing."

"Well I rather fancy doing one with you. It'd make a great lecture - and a good book."

"What sort of river?   I can't do one of those that involves miles of portaging or negotiating great rapids."

"Of course not. I had the Danube in mind. Fascinating, going through several major cultures....."

"Not to mention taking in the whole of Europe. And crossing the Iron Curtain."

"Just think what an adventure that would be."

"Mm, it might if I were a canoeist."

"You *are* a canoeist. Look at all those week-ends we had with the canoe club."

It was true that we had acquired a canoe - a sturdy aluminium Grumman - and had taken part in a number of week-end trips camping and canoeing near Lechlade.

"I don't think you can compare a few miles on the Thames with crossing an entire continent and leaping the political divide in the process."

"I agree the whole thing will take a lot of planning," George conceded.

----oOo----

Yes, it certainly did take a lot of planning, but it was of the kind we both revelled in. Fortunately in the course of my travel writing career, I'd made good contacts with the tourist organisations of many countries, especially in Europe, and especially in eastern Europe.   The Danube passed along or through seven countries, four of which - Czechoslovakia, Hungary, Romania and Bulgaria - then required visas.

The problem was that each country was different with regard to the duration of visas, how long in advance you could apply for them and, once there, where or how often you had to present your passport. In some cases we'd only be able to get the visa once we knew the date of the arrival which, on a journey of this nature, was impossible to predict with precision. I spent several days in London collecting the necessary paperwork as well as information on everything we might need, such as camp sites, rules of the road, rules of the river, locks and dams, maps,

George who loved doing it and was good at it, appointed himself route planner. Maps were spread all over whichever surface was available, as he worked out the best if not the quickest routes to our launching point. Once he looked up from manoeuvring a way through the industrial Ruhr and grunted "Trouble with getting old is that so many place names resonate. I passed over most of these when I was in Bomber Command."

"Perhaps better not mention that if we're camping in the area."

"Hmmm." He gave here one of those grins which reminded me of a small boy caught in some mildly wicked act, or of a deeply familiar friend complicit in some shared experience.

The journey presented no major problems. We had a millpond crossing from Harwich to Hook of Holland, and decided to camp at a site near Arnhem, George musing over the bridge whose taking cost such a spectacular and largely avoidable sacrifice in 1944. We reminded each other that it had taken place only a few months before I'd dived under my eiderdown as the ceiling fell upon me while George was being marched back and forth across a dwindling chunk of Germany.

It was at our first camp we also had an opportunity to check our equipment, finally selected on the basis of discussion and need. George's friend Tom worked on the principle 'if you can't eat it, don't take it', but being new to the game of long distance self-sufficiency, I found quite a few reasons for expanding on such stark restrictions. We were after all on a working trip and needed cameras, film stock, some reference books, a tape recorder. We were bird watchers so needed binoculars. The sleeping bags, cooking equipment and utensils, plastic washing bowl and water containers were incontestable essentials. It proved quite a jigsaw fitting it all into the canoe.

We'd decided to transport the canoe on the roof of the car as we normally did, and drive to the Danube's source at Donaueschingen in the Black Forest. Then we would continue a further 300 km by road to Ulm, which seemed to be the best point from which to start canoeing

81

while avoiding time-taking rapids round which we would need to portage. We would hopefully leave our car at the Canoe Club there from which we would eventually retrieve it at the end of our adventure.

George had already proved his skill at packing for major camping journeys so I left him to it during the week preceding our departure. By the time we were ready to leave, most of the village knew of our venture and quite a few came to see us off. A chorus of *drive carefully* accompanied us as we headed down the road.

Though we had decided right from the beginning to camp wild as much as possible, this did not turn out to be as simple as expected. We weren't much troubled by riverside roads or railways along the upper shores of the Danube, but there were long stretches when, on one or both sides, the natural bank had been built up into a protective dyke. It was impossible to see what lay beyond without stopping to scramble to the top of it. Then, as likely as not, we'd be faced by a sea of nettles and high grass, or some farmer's crop or, if there were a community nearby, a narrow footpath along the top of the dyke bordered by trees or shrubs.

When there was not a dyke, there might be reed beds or a thick growth of shrubs often overhung the water which again needed penetrating to find what lay beyond. It was all rather time-taking and we soon learned to start looking early. When the terrain did seem suitable it was usually a corner of private land, so I learnt a series of comprehensible if ungrammatical phrases for asking permission to camp for one night in all the necessary languages.

For a tent, we settled on a model which had an entrance on two sides, obviating the need for one person to crawl over the other in order to get out. Such inconveniences, of course, didn't apply to large tents but George, who referred to them as jousting tents and did not consider a tent to be a tent if you could stand up in it, would have none of them. The fly-sheet left quite a spacious covered foyer either side between itself and the inner tent, a great boon in wet weather. It also avoided any need to cook in the rain.

For cooking we took two paraffin-burning Primus stoves, a small one of considerable vintage, and a new model that folded into its own case. We kept the smaller stove, together with mugs and the other necessities for making brews through the day, in a tin box that was easily accessible. We also used paraffin for lighting, the lamp's soft glow enhancing many an evening camp. Lamps, canisters and a basic supply of staple needs (rice, instant potato, powdered milk, coffee, tea, some emergency tins, detergent, salt, spices) were stored in a large wooden box that was more or less waterproof and fitted snugly amidships. One small box contained medical supplies and another a sewing kit.

Though it was a while before we became fully aware of it, one of the biggest headaches of the venture was keeping things dry. The cause might be rain, but equally it could be the wash of another boat, or the wind whipping up the surface of the river. It took very little water to create havoc amongst belongings that were limited and therefore all the more precious and, though we took certain precautions, they were rarely enough. One precaution was to cover maps with a transparent film and keep them in a proper map case. Above all we had a spray cover which was rather a pain to fix, leaving me feeling very uneasy that if we should capsize it might be difficult to struggle free.

Overall we spent a phenomenal amount of time unloading the canoe, baling it out and re-loading. It made us very respectful of our predecessors. Almost any early print depicting trade on the Danube featured some version of the waterway's trading vessels. Powered by the current and steered by enormous oars fore and aft, they would set off on the considerable journey from, say, Ulm to Vienna and sometimes even as far as Belgrade. Cargo and passengers were housed in a crude hut built on a platform amidships. Most of the vessels were broken up for their timber when they reached journey's end, since it cost a great deal more to return them upstream than to build a replacement.

Larger and more solid vessels, however, plying the waters from further down river were hauled back by great teams of horses, a procedure complicated by the fact that the *treppelweg* or tow path frequently switched to the opposite bank in order to avoid some topographical obstacle. Thus special 'horse boats' had to be included in the convoy to transport animals and men from one side of the river to the other. In addition, there was a separate kitchen boat to reduce the risks of fire, and a flotilla of smaller boats to hold the tow ropes out of the water and prevent them from fouling. Five dozen horses and half as many men might be involved in these journeys which made ours seem a model of simplicity.

We had calculated that we ought to average around 25 km. each day. This did not sound much, but we had to allow for the time-taking business of shopping, as well as for sightseeing, meal stops and the necessary self-indulgence of simply stopping and staring. There would be the unpredictable and sometimes considerable delays of border formalities from time to time, plus a host of delaying factors that only revealed themselves as we progressed. Our average on actual paddling days, therefore, needed to be half as much again.

So, at 8.30 one May Sunday morning we finally cast our canoe upon the waters of the Danube. Now that the moment had come, the current - about 8 km per hour - appeared alarmingly swift, the canoe very frail, and 2588 km an awesomely long way. These thoughts were so pre-occupying that we had travelled a few hundred metres before I realised it. Not only had the canoe remained intact beneath us, but she felt reassuringly stable. Those first moments were delightful and pretty well effortless. They were also short-lived for within seven kilometres we met our first obstacle At the time there were twenty-one locks between Ulm and Vienna and this was the only one that closed at week-ends, so we were obliged to portage. Happily a week-end fisherman found our labours more intriguing than his unproductive rod and lent us a hand. The first of countless fishermen we were to meet along the Danube, I salute his memory.

In the end, the locks were fun. The early ones were self-operated, with no lock keeper and the instructions of course in German. An all-too-brief crash course on cassettes had left me very conscious of my inadequacy in that language, and one of our last purchases had been a pocket German dictionary. Very early, I found myself frantically leafing through its pages as we rode the current mid-stream, faced by a large sign on the river bank that read *Lebenesgefahr*.

It took a while as there was a lot of text to be deciphered.

"Oh," I said at last. "It means 'danger to life',"

It turned out that this was no more nor less than a warning that there was a lock ahead. Indeed we gradually learned that nearly all river dangers, at least in official eyes, were connected with dams or bridge construction and soon built up an adequate vocabulary to see us through, though it might have limited uses elsewhere.

The dictionary was also useful in sorting out the instructions for lock usage, which involved making sure a lever was in the right position for opening or closing the appropriate gate, then either vigorously turning a handle or simply pressing a button. In most cases we had to fill the lock before we could open the gate just wide enough for our slender craft to slip through. By the time we had done this and then let all the water out again, there was ample opportunity to brew up some coffee in a setting usually attractively landscaped by whatever authority exercised its powers over locks in Germany. With experience we became quite adept at lock procedures and there was some satisfaction at one of the later locks in sharing our new-found knowledge with a couple of puzzled German kayakists who had just joined the river.

With time and experience, my anxiety moderated to quiet satisfaction. It was only a few hundred yards after we launched at Ulm where the current looked alarmingly fast that I realised how stable the canoe felt and that moving with the current made it seem much less daunting.

From time to time we were brought face to face with the river's history.

"Hey, look where we coming to," George said on one occasion, passing me the map.

"Blindheim?" I sounded puzzled.

"Blenheim to us. Battle of... all those men, horses, armaments from all over Europe."

"Not to mention all those corpses. The history books don't tell you what happens to them."

Indeed, the river was a major landmark throughout history. For the Celts, many centuries before Blenheim's battle, the Danube had provided a highway to new territory. For the Romans after them it was a natural defence line against successive waves of barbaric hordes, along the border of their Empire all the way to the Black Sea.

We covered the first 220 miles from Ulm to Passau in ten days and felt pleased with ourselves. Our camp sites ranged from a patch of stubble field to the corner of a waste dump. The scenery varied from pleasant to impressive, the latter as we paddled through the Kelheim Gorge where the current was so fast we hardly needed to make any effort. It was also where we learned how to stop in such conditions. It was necessary to point the canoe at an angle to the current and let the latter ease us into the bank.

Regensburg was the first major town on our route and, beyond it, for the first time we found ourselves sharing the river with considerably more traffic. Much of it, especially at week-ends, took the form of pleasure boats which proved to be more of a menace than the heavier cargo-carrying traffic. In the case of the pleasure craft, their owners seemed unaware of the problems caused by their wash when they came too close. When we signalled at them to go away, they thought we were waving and waved back. The cargo boats were of two kinds: tugboats hauling their fleet of barges like a mother hen clearing a way for her chicks; and more economical push barges, nudging their cargo from behind.

When we reached Passau at the confluence of the Inn, the Ilz and Danube, we decided to stay at the Canoe Club, a stiff upstream one-kilometre paddle up the Ilz, but well worth it for the real beds and unlimited hot water we found at the end of it. Established on the site of a Roman fortress, in turn superimposed on a Celtic settlement, Passau's survival was something of a miracle we discovered after checking the local guide book. In addition to the usual medieval hazards of fire and pestilence, it had also had to cope with earthquake and flood.

"The river is rather high now," the people at the Canoe Club told us, "And there are warnings it will get higher. You must check when you get to Vienna."

The Tourist Office obligingly provided us with a guide on learning that George and I were lecturing/writing on our trip. He took us to the castle museum with superb views over the city, then across the river to the ancient walls and towers of the Innstadt district. Here he paused to point out a waterside dwelling.

"Adolf Hitler lived there for a time as a child," he said. "Once he fell into river, but someone rescued him."

"Were the gods looking the other way that day?" George asked under his breath.

By such miniscule events can the course of history be changed.

----oOo----

There were about 300 km of paddling from Passau to Vienna. One of the first major changes came in the nature of the locks, no longer self-operated but now called *gross-schleuse*, with their attendant flashing lights, control towers and disembodied voices. There were seven of these, some of which we had to share with our increasingly large river companions, and which provided trolleys for sports boats. Going through the actual lock was now quite a daunting experience as the water was lowered and we sank into a dim dankness that rarely saw the sun.

It was some time after Linz that George said, "Mauthausen next stop."

"Oh." I couldn't actually think of anything else to say.

It was an attractive little town, though its fame was not for this but rather for being the site of one of the most awful concentration camps in World War Two. As we approached it, signs of an imminent storm came as no surprise after the heat of several days. We managed to find a wild camp site, unload the canoe, erect the tent and haul the canoe to supposed safety balanced across tree roots before the storm burst. Sometime later, as we lay listening to the tattoo of rain on the tent, we became aware of an alien sound, as of metal knocking against a hard surface. George crawled out into the soggy world.

"That was close," he said on his eventual return. Apparently the front of the canoe having filled with rainwater, the weight had caused it to tip over and slide into the river. He found it banging gently against a rock whose presence had been the only obstacle to prevent it from drifting out into the Danube current - and putting an end to our expedition.

We visited the concentration camp next day.

"It's obscene," I kept saying because I could think of no other word. It was the photographs that made the impression: the ones on the identity cards of the men and women brought in with their well-brushed hair and self-conscious smiles, looking like anyone's cousin or parent; and the later ones in huddled groups in striped prison uniform, or naked in an anonymous pile of corpses.

We walked back in silence to the camp and, although it was only mid-afternoon, decided not to linger. Much of the rest of the way to Vienna had more pleasant associations, in particular three successive and famous stretches, the Strudengau, Nibelungau and Wachau, representing a total of 50 memorable miles of fine scenery. It also provided some good currents, charming small towns and, in the case of the Wachau, famous vineyards and castles.

On the approach to Vienna we became aware that the speed of the current was not due only to local topography.

"The river's much higher," George observed on several occasions. It also bore a growing amount of flotsam ranging from broken branches to whole trees and even the horribly bloated corpse of a pig. The rain continued as we went through the lock at Altenwörth, the last we were to encounter for about 1000 km. The rain continued through our last camp before reaching Vienna. We awoke to find the Danube had risen quite alarmingly close to tent and canoe: something else we would need to watch out for as the river continued to swell.

But before that there was Vienna where life suddenly became very complicated. Clearly we were going to have to spend some time in the Austrian capital. Among other things, we needed now to get our visas for Czechoslovakia. We spent the first morning checking through our belongings, drying what we could and noting, with dismay, that some pages of our passports had become smudged by contact with river and rain. We decided to check with the Czechoslovak Tourist Office.

"Yes," agreed the pleasant lady there. "There may be a problem. I will make an appointment with you at our Embassy."

A Mr Krameš in the Visa Department, who spoke no English, made it blindingly clear that as far as he was concerned, not only were the visas not valid, but the passports were also unacceptable. Astonished, George and I re-examined them - slightly buckled it was true, but with indisputable courtesy requesting that we should be granted passage without let or hindrance, etc. Thumping the passports down on to the table, Mr. Krameš departed effectively ending the discussion.

Chastened, George and I took an expensive taxi to the British Embassy which, blessedly, though officially closed, allowed us in and listened to our sorry tale. The pro-Consul, who remained splendidly unsurprised that two of Her Majesty's citizens had dampened their passports in the Danube, gave out a calm reassurance that was majestic. He then, amazingly, told us that if we cared to return to the Czechoslovak Embassy at 9.30 a.m. next day, he thought we would find everything in order. We did and it was.

Our problems, however, were not over. The river levels had risen so much that officially all traffic on the Danube was prohibited.

"And that includes us," I said firmly, noting George's stubborn expression.

We took the opportunity to explore Vienna's splendours, its museums, art galleries, Opera House, coffee shops where we indulged in its excellent if expensive coffee and pastries, and then moved further out so George could enjoy the *heuriger,* the young wine from the last harvest, and the taverns in which it was served.

Finally the ban on using the Danube was lifted and, after much mopping up, cleaning and re-packing, George and I took to the river once more. There was one more landfall in Austria: at the fine Roman remains of Carnuntum at Petronell. Because of the current we managed to miss the Austrian border crossing at Hainburg, but there was no hue and cry. Soon after crossing into Czechoslovakia, however, a military boat roared out to meet us and to escort us to the necessary landing point in our third Danube country, since divided into the Czech Republic and Slovakia.

We were led to a stretch of river bank where shortly three youngish men arrived to do the formalities, clearly amused by this foreign couple and their mode of transport. In due course we reached Bratislava where the local tourist office were expecting us. The city was not obviously attractive but had a lot of history, including the castle which owed its appearance to the Habsburgs and especially Maria Theresa who had it Baroquised in the late 18th century. There were excellent views of the city and river from the castle, and also from the revolving restaurant atop the high central pylon of the bridge from which the Danube's waters still looked high and fast.

"Isn't this great!" exclaimed George some time after we had left Bratislava and entered the tangled watery wilderness that was the Slovak Danube in flood. The state of the river rendered our good maps of this section almost useless; channels existed where they should not, forming islands that had no right to be there, and many of the recommended sites had simply disappeared under water. On the whole there was an uneasy stillness as though the floodwaters had inflicted some deep wound that had yet to heal.

For a couple of days we had marvellous bird watching and the landscape to ourselves. And then the weather broke and it rained and rained for two-and-a half days. Such unrelieved wetness had a quality of its own, with hour succeeding soggy hour as if it were forever. It was not terribly enjoyable.

"You can't get wetter than wet," observed George.

"But you can get colder," I said. Our eyes became sore from sodden hair dripping into them.

On our last night on the Slovak Danube, we made camp on a grassy meadow. I said jauntily, "You know you can't fully appreciate the normally accepted comforts of life until you have experienced true discomfort," pre-empting one of George's favourite sayings. But I had to acknowledge its truth as we peeled off wet clothing, crept into dry sleeping bags, felt numbness retreat and suffusing warmth transform misery into joy.

It rained all night and next morning. The river was shrouded with mist and we scuttled across to the right bank at the first opportunity, praying that nothing would loom out at us unexpectedly, as we approached country number four.

At the border control at the Hungarian town of Komarom we continued to shiver uncontrollably as our passports were examined and, in due course, a customs officer, came down to subject our canoe to astonished scrutiny.

"You have firearms?" he mimed.

"No," we mimed back, "we have not."

All the same he knelt down and rummaged among our bags and boxes.

"He's looking for a stowaway," George said *sotto voce.*

Back in Passport Control, the officer had drawn, unasked, a sketch map of Komarom on which he had marked shops, banks, travel office and restaurants.

At our first camp in Hungary we were awakened in the middle of the night by loud voices and laughter. Eventually George put his head out of the tent to be greeted by astonished silence from a couple of young soldiers wearing cloaks and wielding beer bottles, one of which was promptly thrust at him.

The next day was miserable too, but the following one brought sunshine and the pleasant small town of Esztergom where we dutifully attempted to register with the police. This proved impossible as we were required to give the camp site at which we were staying, only there wasn't one. We were now approaching the Danube Bend, a beautiful section on the approach to Budapest, and were almost blown round it by an obliging north-easterly wind.

The Hungarian Danube was more attractive than we had anticipated. Of course it was pretty flat but it also had a rural quality that had long disappeared in the West.

----oOo----

Clearly there were far more pairs of eyes looking out for us than we imagined for when we reached Bezdan, the first small community in Yugoslavia, a small reception committee of young men in military and customs uniforms awaited us on the steps by the river, along with about a million mosquitoes. One spoke English and suggested we completed the formalities the next day as the bosses had gone home.

"We do not have Yugoslav money," George said. "Is there a restaurant in the town which will take English?"

"I think so on main square," the English-speaking one said. "But I not wish to know."

It felt that officialdom might prove a little less official in Yugoslavia, as it then was.

At some point next day we filled in a form of great complexity and George agreed he was *commandant de yachte.* Alas, no one translated the form for us which, in due course, almost brought the expedition to an untimely end.

The stretch through Yugoslavia proved to be the most varied. For the first few days we found ourselves crossing the fertile plain of Vojvodina, once an important part of the Habsburg Empire, and home to twenty races and nationalities. It was also the scene of much conflict a decade or so later with the break-up of Yugoslavia. In due course we reached Novi Sad, capital of Vojvodina dominated by Petrovaradin. The fortress was raised by the Austrians in 1740-80, with an unbelievable 77 km of passages burrowing down through eleven underground levels; its sheer size and impregnability earned it the title of the Gibraltar of the Danube. At a jetty across the river, yet another delegation of river police awaited us.

Only fifty or so miles separated Novi Sad and Belgrade where the local tourist office had offered us a room in the splendid Jugoslavija Hotel right on the river. We had good contacts in the Yugoslav capital who soon descended on us to show us the sights and take us to dinner in the Bohemian Skardalija district.

One of the highlights of Belgrade was Kalemegdan, a park round the fortress of the same name towering above the confluence of the Danube and Sava rivers. It was this situation which had made it such a desirable spot and the object of conflict for much of its history. Most of the many surviving structures were Turkish or Austrian, but embedded in them were remnants dating from the early Slavs who called their new city "Beli Grad" ("White City"); and before that the Romans and, earlier still, the Celts.

George and I, and especially I, thoroughly enjoyed our encounter with luxury, I insisting on having two baths a night to make up for those I'd missed. "Can't understand this obsession with cleanliness," George muttered occasionally.

The hot weather we had brought to Belgrade became even hotter, and we were quite glad when it was time to take up our paddles and get back on the river, which was always cooler. The scenery was rural and rolling - little hills that were the outliers of the much sterner heights of the Carpathians and Balkan Range. There were two main historic buildings to see as we progressed towards the Kazan Gorge - the fortress of Smederevo and the castle of Golubac. And, at last, the Kazan Gorge itself, the most stupendous section of the Danube's entire length.

By then the river was providing a frontier between Yugoslavia and Romania, and when some islands materialised it was difficult to know to which country they belonged. To be on the safe side we kept our canoe as close to the right, Yugoslav, bank as possible. By now there was very little current, which was unlikely to improve before we reached the locks known as the Iron Gates at the further end of the Gorge. I was a bit nervous of the Kazan Gorge; it all sounded big and overwhelming, but in the event it was OK since our concentration was entirely on moving forward however slowly.

There was an unspoken worry as to how and where we might land, so it was all the more surprising when we rounded a bend and came upon a scattering of picnickers on a gently sloping meadow. We realised almost immediately that we had reached one of the archaeological highlights of all Europe, the Neolithic settlement of Lepenski Vir dating back to 6000 B.C. In fact, the actual site had been drowned by the flooding created by the construction of the Iron Gates. But the settlement itself had been transferred stone by stone half way up the mountainside.

The vicious wind stayed with us to and beyond the Iron Gates and it was with great relief that we came to the border town of Kladovo. It was immediately obvious there would be no place to camp, but miraculously the manager of Djerdap Hotel offered us a room and a small army of delightful students helped us carry our worldly goods up to our room on the eighth floor.

We had barely completed this when one of the students returned, looking very troubled.

"You must go down," he said. "Immediate. The police ask for you and they are very angry."

Afterwards, George said "I suppose we should have realised that there must be some significance in the interest the river police were showing in us on the early stretches of the Yugoslav Danube."

"Mm, hindsight is a great teacher," I said. "The whole trouble was that no one in those elaborate proceedings where you became 'commandant de yachte' took the trouble to explain that where the river was a frontier between two countries we needed to report each time we landed."

The chief of police at Kladovo was very angry indeed. One of the students who spoke good English came with them to act as interpreter.

"If I come to London Airport and do not go through immigration, they also would be angry," he apparently raged. It seemed unwise to point out the unlikelihood of such a circumstance.

With the help of the students, George and I had humped all our belongings from the eighth floor of the hotel to the river police station, fortunately nearby. The police chief went on ranting for what seemed a long time, but their student interpreter explained with a small smile that it was mostly more of the same. Finally he stopped abruptly, glared at us both in silence and said that, because he understood we were very sorry, we could stay but must report to the police daily. The following evening he turned up in the hotel bar and bought us each a drink, murmuring something which sounded surprisingly like some sort of apology.

"They're quite strange these Slavs," I commented. "But I rather like them."

They were also generous. For the remaining stretch bordering Bulgaria, we were regularly supplied with fish and water melons by fishermen along the shore. There were no further untoward incidents and we reached Ruse in about a week. Ruse was to be the end of our journey for that summer as we had not managed to finalise the arrangements for Romania. The canoe was ceremoniously loaded into the goods carriage of an international train for Western Europe. It disappeared for a while but turned up in Germany and finally Victoria Station some weeks later, complete with the rest of our goods and chattels.

In the meantime we'd completed the arrangements for Romania and the next summer drove all the way back to Silistra the river port in Romania facing Ruse with the canoe on the roof of the car. Compared with the previous summer, it was a relatively short river journey, without any major mishaps though quite a lot of discomfort as there was a shortage of river-side communities along with their welcome wells. The locals drank the river water, but I wasn't ready to put it to the test.

Much of our paddling was through the Delta, the river dividing and rejoining and dividing again in a watery maze. Quite often we found ourselves making little headway through what we came to call Danube soup: a mixture of water lilies and other waterborne vegetation that made us feel as though we were paddling through a field. It led to some magnificent bird watching. On one occasion we nearly bumped our heads on a perching kingfisher who was looking the wrong way; on another occasion, we chanced upon a fleet of eighty storks. Once a white-tailed eagle soared overhead, and for a long stretch there seemed to be a tree-perching hobby every few hundred yards.

Finally we had paddled as far as we could, and to reach the final goal of the Black Sea we hired a fisherman and his boat. He rowed us to a point where only a sandbank separated us from the Black Sea; we landed near it and clambered to the top of the dune to gaze out on the gently heaving brown expanse of our final goal.

"Well, we made it," George murmured, and there wasn't much more to be said. No one was in sight to witness our triumph apart from our fisherman and, for him, it was just another day. Within a couple of days we and the canoe had boarded the regular ferry back upstream to Silistra to rejoin our car for the return home. We did so with a great feeling of achievement.

In our absence a lot had been happening in the Middle East. Iran's Shah had been ousted and the Ayatollah Khomeni returned to Teheran from exile in a surge of fundamentalism. Preoccupied with our own affairs the major import of this did not immediately impinge until it was followed soon after by the American hostage crisis. The world had seemed a good deal less worrying on the waters of the Danube.

1981-84: Big Muddy

While we were canoeing across Europe, Nick and Claire were busy furthering their careers. Nick did some travelling, then went to Bristol University to study philosophy; Claire chose education and psychology and studied at Warwick University. By the time we had launched on our next adventure, Nick had moved to Australia to which he emigrated in due course. Claire took a job with an electronic enterprise where she met her future husband Mike.

Our next adventure began with George asking, "How would you feel about canoeing another big river? I was thinking of the Mississippi. For a start there'd be no language problems."

"Yes I suppose we do speak more or less the same language." I sipped my coffee. "Are you serious?"

"Absolutely. It'll take some planning, given the distance. Not only that, but the river goes through or alongside ten States. And then we'll need to hire a canoe. We could try the American Canoe Union." George went over to the bookcase and came back with the atlas. He *was* serious. I saw the river started close to the Canadian border and flowed through the entire length of the United States. It looked a very long way. At over 4000 km, it was a very long way.

"They call it the Big Muddy over there. But we'll have to miss out some of the earlier stretches to avoid a lot of portaging. For example we can do a token stretch of the headwaters, then put the canoe back in at Minneapolis. After that it's navigable all the way. It'll take time to organise. Two years I estimate."

"So, 1984. Presumably you're not proposing to remain static for two years?"

"When have we ever remained static for two years? Any thoughts?"

"A revisit to Yugoslavia would be useful." I'd recently been asked to update a book on it.

But prior to the Mississippi, other things happened. It was during the early '80s that I became more involved with the Fellowship, doing a stint as secretary of our local group and then becoming our group representative at the local Intergroup. The latter covered a considerable area - Oxfordshire and areas of adjoining counties and all the groups within them. The idea was to meet about every three months to discuss any problems, and find ways of spreading the Fellowship message. The number of groups was growing annually.

It was a very firm part of our policy that we did not advertise ourselves (anonymity was sacrosanct) but attracted by example. It was Intergroup's responsibility to carry this out with the help of groups and, most importantly, to run the telephone service. The aim was to make this available twenty-four hours a day, seven days a week, but of course it depended on finding enough willing volunteers and the money to run it because it was a rigid tenet that in all that it did the Fellowship should be self-supporting, avoiding any outside help which might end up by compromising its hard-won principles.

It was also during this period that I read a great deal about the Fellowship's history, its humble beginnings (with the meeting of recovering alcoholics in the early 1930s), and its hard-earned spread across the world. It reached the U.K. in 1947. Most Intergroups held an annual convention, usually lasting a day. Some regions held longer conventions, lasting a week-end. The first one I went to was on the South Coast and was known as the South of England Convention for which we took over a sizeable holiday camp. I went with two well established members and found it immensely impressive to see so many people and knowing they were all like me. Or rather most of them. There were, of course, members of our sister organisation catering for families, and accordingly a bar to meet their needs; but they were in the minority and to witness the jollity on Saturday night emanating from several hundred sober people was impressive.

----oOo----

Among the major events of the time was the marriage of Prince Charles to Diana Princess of Wales. Much has been made of the romance though, with hindsight, Diana's youth, the 13-year age difference between the two and her general 'un-stuffiness' did not seem to make her the ideal candidate as future royalty in the House of Windsor. And her hounding by press photographers aroused sympathy among most people. Their first son William was born in June, 1982.

We also found ourselves at war a couple of times during this period - the First Gulf War of 1980-81 and the Falklands War of 1982. As for the former, it proved to be the precursor of far worse troubles. It was in the course of exploring the complexities of these that I began better to understand the extent to which today creates tomorrow's history and vice versa. I had tended to assume that Islam had evolved so dramatically, in part, as a challenge to the conflicts developing between Judaism and Christianity in the Middle East. It took a while to understand that Islam, in turn, was no more homogenous than the faiths preceding it: that the beliefs that separated its various followers were just as divisive; and, finally, that the situation had been further compounded, not least at the end of the First World War, when the British and French dismantled the Ottoman Empire leading to borders that would encourage such great hatred decades later.

Nevertheless there were some, if rather brief, successes. The French Mandate of Lebanon which declared itself an independent Lebanon in 1943, became not only economically successful, even gaining a reputation as the Switzerland of the Middle East, but briefly flirted with an unusual degree of tolerance by electing to choose a Christian President, a Shia Moslem Speaker of Parliament, a Sunni Moslem Prime Minister and a Greek Orthodox Deputy Prime Minister. Such common sense was not long lasting as bitterness between warring factions in neighbouring countries spilled into Lebanon. A major effect was the rising power of the Shia Hezbollah backed by Iran in the ongoing conflict with Israel. By 1975 it had descended into an ongoing civil war lasting until1990, costly in both economic and human terms.

As for the Falklands, I was never convinced that the cause justified the loss of life once you delved into the history of it since several countries seemed to have had a stake in them. In particular tensions over their ownership had simmered for a very long time between Britain and Argentina. Early under Margaret Thatcher's premiership, at a time of budget cuts, there had even been thoughts of transferring their sovereignty to Argentina. Then the latter invaded the islands in April, 1982, and war was declared.

Unfortunately during this period, I also had a return of my depression. In fact it had come back even earlier and I had moaned bitterly that this was in spite of doing all the 'right things' like embracing sobriety. My then-doctor put me on tranquillisers which appeared to do the trick, though I knew the Fellowship frowned upon any drugs that could be classed as addictive. The tranquillisers worked but not permanently and when the depression returned I was reluctant to go back to them. The symptoms of depression are extremely unpleasant and difficult to explain to anyone who has not experienced them. The nearest I can get is to a sense of fear for which you can find no grounds but which is so strong it dominates all other thought.

"Do you think we could stop for a while," I asked George as we wound our way up a narrow road in Yugoslavia's Velebit mountains.

He stopped at the first lay-by. "What's up?"

Having observed me trying to force food down at countless meals and struggle out of grey worlds, he accepted that I was suffering from something which he did not fully understand.

"When we get back you must go to the doctor and get this sorted once and for all." Alas, I didn't think this was likely, but agreed I needed to do something.

George's voice took on a lighter note as he said, "Look, there's a raptor. Left of that summit at about one o'clock." He had discovered that one of the quickest ways of temporarily jerking me out of depression was bird-watching, something I had taken up in sobriety and which we both enjoyed. It became a constant feature of our daily lives, whether observing through the kitchen window or on any travels.

On my return home I did make an appointment, with a different G.P. as the earlier one had left. This one ('*call me Hugh*') quizzed me on my depression and the alcoholism I admitted to. Finally he said, "I think we'll try you on a course of antidepressants."

"I don't want anything addictive," I said quickly.

When it became clear that I was serious in my reluctance, Hugh raised a quizzical eyebrow. "Do you want to get better or don't you?"

I agreed that I did. He went on, "These will probably make you feel worse before you feel better so I don't think you'll find them addictive. Come back in a month - or before if necessary."

He was right. The antidepressants did make me feel worse, but it was somehow acceptable when you knew there was a legitimate reason. By the time I saw him again I thought there was an improvement and, in due course, I was able to reduce my daily intake of medication.

I also became more involved in the Fellowship and was sent as a representative of our region to the annual conference in Manchester at which all matters were discussed that might improve the spreading of our message. So all in all, it was a crammed summer, but as the result of a mammoth effort, I managed to meet the deadline for the Yugoslav book revision.

On our return we also found that the replies had begun to come through from America, and they were not exactly encouraging. Minnesota informed us, *that the Mississippi is a large and dangerous river carrying heavy river traffic and with unpredictable currents.* Tennessee wrote *In the unlikely event of you reaching Memphis you will be made very welcome.*

Then one day I answered the phone to a pleasant trans-Atlantic voice which informed me that it represented the American Canoe Union and understood that we required the loan of a canoe. They would be delighted to provide a Wenonah manufactured in Minnesota. I expressed profound gratitude and was about to ring off when the voice asked, "Oh by the way, would you also like paddles?" I agreed that these would be very useful indeed, grinning as I replaced the receiver.

----oOo----

A few months later, beside a bridge of stepping stones across a shallow stream, I re-read the words on a post: *Here 1475 feet above the ocean, the mighty Mississippi begins to flow on its winding way 2552 miles to the Gulf of Mexico."*

"Our encyclopaedia says 2340 miles."

"They've straightened out some of the curves," said the American friend who had come to the headwaters with us."

George was busy trotting back and forth across the stepping stones, hands deep in pockets, with a hunched up look of suppressed excitement more appropriate to a truant school boy than a lecturer in his mid-sixties. We had settled for paddling the first 65 miles of the headwaters, after which we would return to Minneapolis to tackle the remainder of the Big Muddy. We had also collected our Wenonah canoe from the rather formidable lady who was its local agent. She watched us paddle a stretch of the river, getting accustomed to the light if rather bouncy vessel.

"Think we'll make it?" George asked.

She was silent for a while. "Guess you might," she said.

For the first hours, the young Mississippi was a fairly indeterminate waterway meandering across a marshy plain. In fact, it was quite difficult to discern the current until we noticed the wild rice growing in it and simply followed the way it was leaning. In due course, the embryo Mississippi shrank to within its own defined banks.

And then, rounding a bend we found our way blocked by a shaggy construction of branches, twigs and mud that spanned the river from bank to bank. Nosing into it we admired our first beaver dam. It proved solid enough to stand on and, in due course, with much heaving and shoving we managed to haul the canoe across the dam with a minimum of downloading. The novelty was beginning to wear off after three dams and we were approaching our fourth when we heard voices behind us. Four men in two aluminium canoes appeared round a bend, paddles raised in greeting. We watched admiringly as they paddled furiously until they were balanced across the beaver dam; then the rear man moved forward and they both bounced up and down until the canoe tipped over the other side. Clearly, with our precious load, this was not a procedure we could emulate.

"Where you guys heading?" one of the men called.

"Bemidji," George called back, clearly no more convinced than I was of our final destination at that moment.

We caught up with them at the next camp site and confessed our true destination, to be greeted by cries of envy. That night we heard coyotes howling in the distance.

Those first four days were idyllic in terms of solitude and surroundings. Then we drove back to Minneapolis with the canoe on the roof of the car and made preparations for the true journey ahead. Our American friends took us and the canoe to put in at Lake Pepin, a considerable widening of the river to lake-like proportions. There we had our first taste of paddling against a strong wind and the tent collapsing on us in the middle of the night; appropriate tent pegs immediately went on the shopping list.

Next day we had our first encounter with river traffic: a great expanse of fifteen barges nudged along by a push boat. And soon after we experienced our first lock. There were twenty-nine of these on the Upper Mississippi and we now had the navigation maps on which they, along with much else, were marked. The locks were huge, but even then the tows had to divide in two in order to get a push boat and all its barges through. At the fourth dam, we waited several hours before making a concerted dash to get to the lock before the next barges appeared.

The lock keeper peered down at us. "What were you guys waitin' for? It's first come first serve with the locks," and so we learned that an 18-ft canoe had priority over the massive cargo loads if it got there first.

On one occasion we chose not to go through a dam but to portage into the channels or sloughs that wound through small islands alongside the main river. It was time-taking and hard work and it was during the process that I noticed the darkening sky.

"Looks as though a storm is brewing."

"If there's a storm coming, get off that river," everyone had warned us.

By the time we'd reloaded and pushed off into the sloughs, the sky was spitting and the wind rising. Soon the wind was a gale against us and the rain increased to a steady downpour, then torrent, then back to steady downpour. It was difficult to see where we were going and, with the river high, there was no chance of camping on the islands. After what seemed an age, George said "Ah!" and steered towards a shore where we landed by a sign that said "No Camping". We decided that in no way and under such circumstances did this apply to us. There was a railway line just above us, along which mile-long cargo trains chugged intermittently through the night.

It was also our first experience of the changing moods of the river. After a night of downpour and gales we awoke to sunshine, and an utterly benign Mississippi.

"Hypocrite," I told it. But we were learning to appreciate the river in its better moods, the mainly rural settings, the river traffic, and especially the riverside people. They really were special, loving our accents, wanting to know more about our travels, amazed by our ambition. Quite often they would take us home and feed us, even offer overnight accommodation. Then there was the girl at a marina who lent us a car to go shopping as it would be "quite a ways to walk". Another girl working in a bar confided she was expecting a baby "on Christmas day. December 25th." She hesitated, then asked, "Is that the same where you folks come from?"

At Davenport, we coincided with July 4th celebrations and sold tee shirts for charity while an impressive and very long parade unfolded through the town. At Burlington, we coincided with Riverboat Days where Civil War battles were re-enacted and we were delegated to camp with the Confederate Army, each member of which mirrored a real person or a family member. After pounding each other, there was much jocularity over a shared barbecue in the evening. At Nauvoo we stayed with a charming Mormon family, in Hannibal we explored the world of Tom Sawyer and Huckleberry Finn, and in between learned some more about the Mississippi's violent weather.

And so we came to St. Louis: gateway to the West for the early settlers, gateway to the South for me. It also proved to have another significance. Before he'd even seen the river traffic, George had suggested that it would be wonderful to get a lift on a tow for a while. With that in mind we'd corresponded with the Missouri State Tourist Department and been given the name Wally Rice, a director of one of the push-boat companies.

"Hi," he said, when we called him. "That's a great thing you two Brits are doing. Let's have lunch and talk."

Wally turned out to be another of those who wished he were coming with us. He explained he could offer us a lift to Memphis depending on the vessels' schedules. We were currently staying in a hotel where we saw ourselves on television being interviewed by a young reporter who rounded off by wishing "that elderly British couple all the best for the rest of their journey."

"Dammit!" muttered George. "I doubt he could paddle across a village pond."

We spent our time sightseeing until the call came from Wally that we should be down by the river that afternoon. Willing arms transferred the canoe and all our belongings from the tug on to the *m.v. Robert Crown* midstream as we travelled alongside each other down the river, and then we stepped from one deck to another ourselves.

We were enthusiastically greeted by the crew, Captain Kenny Dae, and eventually Ida, the cook, whose figure paid tribute to the excellence of her cooking. She greeted us with "Y'all want coffee? It's brewin' all day and all night. My boys make sure of that." 'Her boys' were the deck hands who spent their duty hours checking the connections that held the barges together.

There followed three blissful days of relaxation, comfort and air conditioning. We spent most of them on the bridge, fascinated by this new view of the river and the techniques used. The procedure was to point their huge expanse of barges towards the far shore of the bend, which could be up to 180 degrees, and then put the engine into reverse letting the current gradually nudge the push-boat and its load round the curve. But it was at night that the river was at its most magical. Then only the cargo boats were on the move their searchlights sweeping across the water from bank to bank.

We now began to see major changes in the river. Further north the Mississippi had been contained between bluffs, controlled by locks and dams and featured small thriving communities. Now it was increasingly contained between high levees, and beyond them a no-man's-land of rough growth beyond which were more levees. The number of communities gradually decreased. This was due to the massive floods that had taken place in earlier times as, with fearful regularity, the Mississippi burst its banks and sent its swollen waters to drench thousands of square miles of the southern States.

And then we crossed from Kentucky into Tennessee. Ida was making up lists of stores she needed for Kenny to radio her requirements through to the marine supply service. "I'll sure miss y'all," she told me. "It was great to have another woman on board. Mebbe one day I'll be calling y'all from some place in one of your shires," she added a little wistfully. And I hoped she would.

We left the *Robert Crown* midstream as we'd boarded her, stepping on to a tug from Waterways Marine Inc. that had eased alongside at matching speed. There was swift, brawny activity as crates of Ida's groceries and mechanical hardware for Jake were exchanged for our canoe, its load and us. Amongst the clutter of cables on the wharf of Waterways Marine a reception committee awaited: a TV crew, radio reporter and a beaming welcome from Sharon, our pretty, intelligent and black guide. The Americans were good at making you feel important.

As soon as we'd checked in to our hotel, we took Sharon out for a coffee. She told us she was a real cocktail, half black, quarter Cherokee, quarter German. She had two sons, one blacker than she was, the other as fair as any German.

"Is there much social mixing? I asked.

Sharon gave a small frown. "We work together, joke together, study together and all that stuff. But really socialise, no. Well, of course there are exceptions; may be quite a lot. Sure you see blacks and whites in the same theatres, hotels, restaurants, but it's not too often you see them at the same table."

We had an invitation to Graceland, the 18-room mansion set in 14 acres that had become a shrine to millions of Elvis Presley worshippers, and were grateful that we did not have to join the considerable queue. It was in appalling taste. The music room was dominated by a huge 24-carat gold-leaf concert grand piano. There was a jungle room full of ersatz animal skins, spears and dark green carpet covering most of the walls, ceiling and floor. In the basement TV Room a mirror ceiling reflected blue clouds on bright yellow walls and the three 25-inch television screens built into one of them so that the King of Rock 'n' Roll could watch three programmes at once. Out in the car port Elvis' mother's pink Cadillac stood among a fleet of shiny cars and flashy motorbikes.

I asked Sharon what she thought and she didn't hesitate. "He left his music and that's *great*; it kinda gave a whole generation a new identity, and that's the one I grew up in. And he was s-o-o-o generous. Would see a poor old woman on the street and give her a Cadillac." Only I heard George musing whether a poor old woman on the street really wanted a Cadillac.

In complete contrast, we visited Mud Island where, on a 50-acre slab of once weed-infested land, the exceptionally good Mississippi Museum had been created. It included a River Walk along a replica of the 1000 miles from Cairo to New Orleans. We strolled along its miniscule waters, stepping over New Madrid's 20-mile bend. A stone's throw away, the Big Muddy herself rolled implacably on to disappear round one of her innumerable meanders as we would next day. But first, on our last evening, we went to the old cotton warehouse that had become Blues Alley. Here, Ma Rainey II and Little Laura Duke, both long past retirement age, expressed love and jealousy, laughter and aching nostalgia with every fibre of their venerable beings. We left emotionally drained.

But Memphis hadn't quite finished with us. A message scrawled in pencil was attached to our canoe next morning. *Dear Intrepids,* it read, *have just completed a solo canoe journey of 6,700 miles. It would be good to talk. You'll find me on the* Connie Mays *at the Lone Star Cement Wharf next door.*

We found Ted - a lean, weathered and bearded British-born Australian - cabinet making on board the *Connie Mays.* Solo, he had canoed the Mississippi system, paddling from the source of the Milk River in Montana's Glacier Park to join the Missouri and thence the Mississippi down to New Orleans and finally along the man-made Intracoastal Waterway into Texas. All told it took a year and a half.

He had plenty of advice for us. "Carry plenty of water - it can get *hot* out there." He thought for a moment. "Have you got boots?" We hadn't. "No, well take a stick along. Some of the snakes aren't too friendly if you tread on 'em by mistake."

----oOo----

There were seventy-three miles of river to Helena, Arkansas, and our next point of contact with humanity. We estimated it would take three days and took provisions for four. It was, as yet, the longest period when there would be no possibility of pulling in to a small-town supermarket or riverside tavern for the delights of iced drinks and air conditioning.

Now, the navigation channel took up most of the river's width and we kept eyes and ears focussed on the potential thrum that meant an approaching vessel. A series of storms had freshened the air and the breeze was fair. The current was fair, too, and despite a late start we did an easy 20 miles before pitching up on a sand bar. All the same there were few moments when we were not profoundly aware of the river's changed moods or learning something new about its behaviour.

Even the currents were different, and sometimes extremely odd. We learned to know where the fast water was: on the outside of the interminable bends, or more or less down the middle of the rare straight stretches. At times the water almost came to a standstill and it felt as though we were paddling through treacle as we crept round the sand bars sprawling out far from the shore almost to the opposite bank.

But what gave us our most testing times were the jagged rocks of the dykes designed to steer the current into the navigation channel. North of St Louis they had all been submerged. Now they were all completely or half exposed, and the latter were far more trying as they were impossible to see from the low level of a canoe. Of course the charts marked their position, but not always their length. On the third day we encountered one that was not marked at all. Later the Corps of Engineers agreed that it had only just been constructed, confirming the need to have the very latest chart. I was the first to notice the tell-tale irregular white ridge of water rocks.

"We'll head up and midstream," George said tersely and with every ounce of strength we did just that. The current was fast and now the roar of water and the sight of the cauldron foaming viciously over jagged rocks became very alarming indeed.

"We won't do it," I whimpered, already anticipating the physical pain of the last moments before oblivion.

Then the nearest rocks slid by within centimetres, and noticeably began to recede. In due course we had another full-blooded Mississippi storm and more than a fair share of headwinds. After that Helena seemed the most desirable place on earth.

Accustomed to the busy little marinas of the Upper River we could be forgiven for not easily identifying the deserted and steep muddy embankment as Helena's equivalent. But as far as I was concerned it had all the attributes of paradise as we hauled the canoe out and squelched up the slope to the little shack that served as a tavern. Half an hour later a young woman approached. "Hello, I'm Maureen Jones, and you'll be staying with us," she said in tones that unmistakeably originated from the Home Counties.

A burly man in jeans appeared carrying some of our mud-spattered gear. "Bill Brothers," he said, "Just came down to make sure y'all doin' fine. Hi Maureen. Take care of 'em."

It seemed Bill was a Big Cheese in Helena and had arranged a party for us the next evening. So we were caught up in another whirl of activity, taken sightseeing, delivered back in time to change for Bill's party. We found ourselves being handed from one group to another: "Hi, I'm Martha (or Janet or Mary Ann) and this is my husband James (or Matt or Eddie). We're so excited to meet y'all."

Among them was Tom, a director of the nearby National River Academy where young people wanting to work on the tows could learn all aspects of river skills. "Drop in for a meal," Tom said, "Or stay the night. You can't miss it."

We noticed for the first time that segregation between the races was quite marked. Indeed the only black with whom we had close contact was Willy, the Brothers' old retainer, as wrinkled as a prune. She reportedly told Bill's wife "Ain't folks just the same wherever they from? That English couple seem real frien'ly, tho' I can't unnerstan' a word they say!"

We got off to a late start so decided to take Tom up on his offer. However from a canoe, one stretch of sand dune or levee covered with bushes or cottonwood trees looks much like another; in the end we decided to take a chance, scrambled up the revetment and made our way across an endless acreage of soya beans towards lights, with dusk falling fast.

As we were having an early breakfast next morning, the Coast Guard arrived. "Anyone know anything about some canoeists?" he asked. We looked at each other with deep foreboding. "Praise be y'all are OK. But your canoe was found upside down an' bin taken back to Helena along with some stuff they found floating in the river...."

It could have meant the end of the expedition. Back at the main marina in Helena, we found joyously that our aluminium box had lived up miraculously to its waterproof promises. The tent, a box of soggy comestibles and a number of other items had also been picked up. My rucksack and the paddles were missing. The latter could be replaced, but the rucksack contained some medication and my wedding ring. Bill Brothers breezed in, hugged us, said "Y'all stay in our guest house as long as you want."

We spent the morning at Helena marina's office, discussing the situation, listing missing items, drinking countless cups of coffee. Towards the end of the morning, the marina manager answer the phone, held it out to me. "Call for you," he said. "Some fisherman's found a rucksack."

"Found a rucksack with some kind of medicines in it," a man's voice said. "Oh, and there was a ring."

I stammered out my thanks. "It's a pleasure ma'am," the voice said. "It may take me a whiles to get to Helena - my wife, she took all the clothes to wash and they're just drying now."

I burst into tears.

The Brothers were so kind. In the end Bill took us and our paraphernalia to Greenville, over the bridge and across the old flood bottomlands of Mississippi State, locally known as the Delta which, indeed, they probably once formed. What they represented in historic terms were some 7,000 square miles, and in economic terms huge areas of cotton and soya bean.

In Greenville Jenny, our pretty mentor from the local Chamber of Commerce, had arranged yet another welcoming party for us. Eliminating a cut-off, the Corps of Engineers had left the town five miles off the main river and it had turned into a fine slack water harbour with dozens of towboat companies and boat building and repair yards lining the shore. Now, thirty towboat companies had shrunk to ten as big investment companies priced the smaller river companies out of the market, then bought 'em up.

"So what happens now?" George asked.

Our guide shrugged. "Now the railroad companies want to buy in, which hasn't been allowed before. According to them we've bin havin' it real easy on the river - free use of them expensive locks and all the money that goes to stop her breakin' loose. But you don't hear 'em braggin ' about all them mineral rights they're sitting on." He grinned. "I guess nothin' ain't simple when it comes to that river."

We did a big supermarket shop before Jenny drove us to the marina where we had left the canoe. After a longish interlude off the river, my old anxieties were returning. With relief I emerged from dark thoughts to find that at least the canoe and the river were in harmony. For the next three hundred miles at least we could be confident that camping problems were over. Ideally we could expect a sandbar, giving easy access to the forest rim beyond. Trees gave the double advantage of shade and protection from wind. For practical purposes the tent needed to be pitched as near as possible to the canoe which, once unloaded, was turned upside down. We'd soon learned that the most placid evening could give way to a night of deluge.

All the same, some of those evenings were near perfection. Then the tent and canoe became our little pocket of civilisation in a world totally dominated by the river. Occasionally a small fishing boat would buzz past, or a motor launch rising high at the head of its own trail of turbulence. But our most constant companions were the push boats, remote in their preoccupation with the narrow thread of the navigation channel. With dusk, the shore markers began winking out their port and starboard messages to the throbbing black shapes whose search lights flickered over the tent from time to time.

Sometimes we'd spare a thought for our predecessors on the river. The most primitive of them had been the ark, little more than a raft with a rudimentary shelter built on it 'amidships'. The more substantial flat boat was essentially a cargo carrier for anything from flour and furs to lumber and lead, cotton and cattle to salt and slaves. Then there was the keel boat which gave rise to the gaudiest, bawdiest stories. Up to 120 feet long, it needed a crew of 8-15 men to control it downstream and more than double that to negotiate the return trip. In the riverside ports along the way, saloons, bordellos and gaming house blossomed to cater for their favourite entertainments. For us these sandy ports of call had more peaceful distractions: a variety of waders or skeins of wood storks, early migrants on an age-old route across the continent.

More substantial ports of all could be numbered on the fingers of one hand between Memphis and Baton Rouge. Happily our contacts had made arrangements for us to be looked after at two off-river communities to break up the longer stretches.

We were directed to pull in at a specified barge terminal on the river bank from which we telephoned to announce our arrival. The first of these was Lake Providence, where we pulled up on the muddy banks beneath Lake Providence Port Elevator. We were duly collected by a slender woman called Gayle Brown. In minutes we were driving into town.

"Good Lord," exclaimed George moments later as Gayle smiled and slowed down so we could fully appreciate the message in flashing lights that winked out from a screen in front of a bank on Main Street: ... *17th August... Louisiana welcomes British canoeists George and Sylvie... temperature 94 degrees F.... 17th August.... Louisiana welcomes British canoeists.....*

"We're having a little party later," Gayle said. Surprise, surprise!! There was indeed a party with a magnificent cake with our names and a picture of a canoe in icing. We felt our egos inflating.

As we left the next morning, a haze soon developed into a grey shroud across the opposite bank, and worryingly reducing visibility up and downstream. It was also then that we hit our first boils, phenomena about which we had been warned very early on. Alarmed by the sound of them, I'd looked out for them anxiously during the early weeks, but when they didn't materialise, forgot about them. Until now. Their cause was the passage of fast water over some irregularity in the river bed. The effect was impressive as the water erupted explosively and without warning into raised "boils", often many yards across. Disconcertingly the canoe veered and swung at the river's bidding.

"So how do we get out of this?" I wailed.

"Just sit tight," George said, infuriatingly calm.

He was right. Here was a danger that was more apparent than real. With its shallow draft the canoe skimmed out almost as quickly as it was drawn into these excrescences.

"This darned river," I complained. "Earlier on it was impossibly wide. Now it's impossibly narrow."

It was true. At times the sand banks sprawled out from the inner curve of almost every serpentine bend, the river barely straightening from one before launching into the next. Sometimes they sprawled so far that the river was squeezed into a deep swift stream just wide enough for the navigation channel, hard up against the revetment on the opposite shore.

Our next major port was Vicksburg which, thanks to the efforts of the Corps of Engineers, lay about a mile up the Yazoo river. It was a hard slog against the current but we'd decided this site of major Civil War action deserved at least a three-night stop, and the prospect of that was enough to add extra strength to my elbow power.

"The great irony," our mentor Benita told us as we looked on the distant glint of the Big Muddy from a hill by Vicksburg, "is the river did by itself what General Grant and all his Unionist forces couldn't figure how to do."

109

In fact, as she pointed out, had the river done its deed a mere thirteen years earlier, there would have been no need for the Siege of Vicksburg, no resulting 22,000 military dead, no starving or diseased civilians, no devastated town.

The siege of Vicksburg began on May 18th, 1863, and lasted 47 days. The Unionist troops dug themselves in among a network of trenches below the hill town, and inch by inch continued to dig their way further up the slopes. Eventually the two armies were so close that when firing ceased in the evenings the soldiers from either side exchanged jokes or sought news of friends and relatives until the mutual massacre resumed next morning. As food and water ran out, the besieged Confederates, soldiers and citizens, eked out dwindling supplies of rancid bacon and musty pea flour with mule meat. As the bombardment intensified they burrowed caves in hillsides. Contemporary diaries give graphic accounts of the conditions though little is said of what happened to the slaves.

We soon realised that if anyone here referred to a war there only had been one war. 'Antebellum' (pre-war) meant only one thing: pre-Civil War. Thus south of Memphis really fine antebellum houses were major features: large and extravagant, they combined various features of European architectural styles: Colonial, Georgian but, above all, Greek Revival with gracious porticos and airy galleries.

Just a few paddling days south of Vicksburg, we came to Natchez, perhaps the doyenne when it came to antebellum houses.

"They say," our guide told us as she drove us deftly around, "that at one time Natchez had more millionaires than New York. No, more. They did not survive the effects of the Civil War, though many of their houses did in various states of repair. Then roads and motorised traffic brought a more lucrative invasion. Natchez rediscovered her heritage and, as someone wryly put it 'opened her doors to the Yankee dollar'."

Most of the fine homes, once repaired, became museums or offered bed and breakfast.

While we were in Natchez, the Mississippi Queen called - the modern sister ship to the Delta Queen. She sat there looking rather like a floating Holiday Inn with a stern wheel stuck on the back. That evening as we sat over a catfish dinner, watching the sun go down in a blaze of glory, George prodded at the map. "I suggest we leave the main river just after Baton Rouge and follow a main distributor down to the Gulf. There won't be much current but we'll be travelling through the heart of real delta country."

I looked at the innocuous blue line representing Bayou Lafourche and an almost straight route into the Gulf of Mexico and agreed it was a fine idea. But first the Big Muddy was to present us with a couple of major tests before Baton Rouge. Not so very many miles south of Natchez, the sand bars that had provided us with so many magical nights suddenly ran out. Now the river banks alternated between steep revetment and low cliffs of soft soil under an overhang of shrubbery. And then in the distance the sky growled, and quite soon the growling became less distant.

"We ought to get off the river," I said. We'd just entered a long straight stretch unhelpfully called Dead Man's Bend.

Finally we could delay no longer. We stepped out of the canoe sinking almost to our knees in mud but, with energy born of desperation, hauled the canoe out of the water, unloaded the camping gear and pitched the tent. The rain started as we shoved in the final pegs. Fortunately at that stage there was little wind and still daylight of sorts.

When the ground sheet began to sink as water started to flow under the tent, George crawled out of the tent before I could stop him. He couldn't hear my "What are you *do*ing?" but I saw he had dug a trench curving above the tent and then down either side of it. Already twin torrents scurried along it carrying the water away from our tiny refuge. Then George shouted something and headed for the river, ignoring my yells of protest. Crouching in the tent entrance I watched him flounder through the mud, haul the canoe further up on the shore, wedge the painter under stones, secure items we'd abandoned. Behind him the river was like molten lead. Fork lightning ripped along it in jagged, lunatic procession in fearsome concert with the detonating sky. It was terrible but also, finally, hypnotic and rather beautiful.

Our next potential problem lay only twenty miles downstream. During her restless history, the Big Muddy's relationships with her tributaries and distributaries had changed dramatically, but never more dramatically than with the Atchafalya over a period of 200 years. It was clear that the Mississippi's shortest and quickest route to the Gulf of Mexico was by the Atchafalya, and left to her own devices there would be no stopping her. On our charts the message was spelt out in red: "very dangerous currents ... amber light indicates structures operational .... vessels should navigate as close to the left descending bank as safety will permit."

In the event it was a bit of a damp squib. There were no amber lights, the current was brisk but manageable, and across the river we could see the Corps of Engineers' rescue vessel just beyond the entrance to the Outflow Channel.

"Ice" George said cryptically, and steered us towards it. The crew, surprised and delighted to have unexpected visitors with strange accents, refilled our water containers, plied us with coffee and a hot meal, and send us off with a box of cookies.

The main feature of the next day was the Angola Landing and its ferry crossing to the Louisiana State Penitentiary The prison buildings lay invisible behind acres of bottomlands swamp and forest and a double line of levees. All the same an official boat roared across to take a closer look at us. Finally, a couple of days later we entered the last long straight stretch before the landing at St. Francisville where we were to be met. It was as hot and airless as it had ever been, but then suddenly we were there at a ferry crossing, hauling the canoe up on a muddy shore. To our astonishment a voice, god-like, came from the sky.

"Are y'all the British guys we've bin waitin' for? We bid y'all welcome."

We'd made it. Well almost.

----oOo----

Within a few days we'd made the transition from big river to the narrow canal of Bayou Lafourche. "Y'all a goin' to have a great time," they assured us at the Louisiana State Tourist Department in Baton Rouge. "The people along those bayous are real special - I guess you know about the Cajuns?" Yes, we did. They were the descendants of French-speaking Arcadians who had drifted south after deportation by the British from Nova Scotia in the 1750s.

"Not one of our greatest moments of glory," George murmured.

Friendly arms helped to launch the canoe and then wave us off. With virtually no current, it was a bit like paddling through treacle.

I watched a piece of flotsam creep along the bankside. "Heavens. I said. At this rate we should reach the Gulf in a couple of weeks!"

And there was another factor we'd not allowed for. Bayou Lafourche was also known as the world's 'longest street'. All along it on either bank were dwellings and backyards, marinas or shopping malls or the Evangelical Church of This or That. All the same, we paddled for a long time in appreciative silence, enjoying the lack of traffic, noise, hustle and bustle. Once we were accosted by someone on a bridge. "Where y'all going?" he called. And now, without fear of sounding boastful, we could say 'the Gulf of Mexico.'

In the end I was the one to find a solution to the camping problem. "I'll knock on the door and ask if we can camp."

We chose the yard carefully, making sure there was an adequate flattish area and not too much adjacent growth in which insects or other creatures might lurk. A lady with a blue rinse opened the door to my gentle tap. and I said my piece. "Y'all would be so welcome," Blue Rinse said. "And, gee, isn't that a British accent?"

I admitted that it was and Blue Rinse turned to call "Honey, come right out and meet our British visitor," and a pleasant-looking man came out to shake my hand vigorously.

Before we knew it, a local reporter had arrived to interview us, and we were promised a real American breakfast next morning. The gambit was so successful that we repeated it. One young lady, living in a caravan above a shore line fringed with cypress trees, actually thanking us for "choosing my yard". Then there was Rebecca Swanner whose husband was in oil, like most of the men in the neighbourhood. Rebecca had befriended a pair of ducks who set up home in her yard and in due course produced a clutch of babies.

"The babes started disappearing," she told us, "then I saw an alligator grabbing one of *my* little ducks out of *my* yard and slinking back into the bayou. It was real terrible. So I called the Wild Life and Fish Refuge, who said no way no could I shoot a protected animal outa season. Who's gonna protect my ducks I demanded? So in the end they sent a guy round to get the old devil."

Alligators began to feature quite a lot in conversations, and this brought us in contact with Annie Miller. Then in her seventies she had built up a profound knowledge of the flora and fauna of the delta and created a rapport with alligators that made her a legend far beyond the frontiers of Louisiana. Indeed, she called them by name. Alligator hunters had developed some unpleasant techniques which included suspending raw chicken from overhanging branches. The meat contained a hook and, thus trapped, the alligator was a sitting target when the hunter came to check his bait. I believe the alligators are now protected, but at that time Annie's mission in life was to bring so much raw meat to feed them that they would not be tempted by the hunters' baits.

As we progressed south, the bayou widened and the thick vegetation was replaced by tall grasses and reeds characteristic of the marshes. It also became busier. Fairly soon we passed our first shipyard and from then on boat building, commercial wharfs, jack-up barges, crew boats for the oil rigs, pleasure launches, skiffs became increasingly our companions. Then there was the shrimping fleet, which developed into a colourful collection of all sizes from skiffs that went out for the day to larger vessels with trawls or 'butterflies' that might be out for up to three weeks.

We also had our first close contact with the Cajuns, who had drifted here when dispossessed by the British when they refused to bear arms against their compatriots in Nova Scotia. This remote corner of Louisiana was already populated by the French and, among the older generation, an old fashioned French was still spoken by them.

Finally we reached Golden Meadow, our last port of call where the police were waiting to man-haul the canoe and our gear on to dry land for the last time. For the next few days we ranged the strange world of the delta that was neither entirely land nor entirely sea. And, at last, we were driven to New Orleans where the canoe was 'moored' next to America's most ostentatious cars in the garage of the Royal Sonesta Hotel on Bourbon Street.

There was an international fair on in the city. We roamed its streets, explored its restaurants and museums and took a chair lift to ride high over 'our' river. Finally the local agents for the canoe company came to collect the canoe. We stood on the sidewalk, hand in hand, watching it retreat down Bourbon Street, below a huge statue of Elvis Presley put there in preparation for that evening's block party. George squeezed my hand. I opened my mouth, changed my mind and closed it again.

No, I wasn't going to admit just then that there was something like a lump in my throat.

1985-1994: reunions

It was a few months after our Mississippi adventure that George asked me on my return from a meeting one evening, "Are you doing anything on the last week-end in May?"

"I can't think of anything. Why?"

"Just had phone call from Julian and Carol. Apparently they want us to come over on that day and meet Adrian and family who will be staying with them."

There was a small astonished silence before I said, "Good God!"

"Yes," George agreed. "I think even He might be surprised."

"I don't think it's a summons we can ignore," I continued. "I wonder what brought it on."

Adrian worked in the Civil Service and we had heard through the family grapevine that he had married and had two daughters. We discovered eventually that his never-met daughters had expressed puzzlement as to why they had never seen their grandfather.

I confess to feeling nervous at the prospect. Though I knew George's marriage had failed long before I came on the scene, I suspect that I was nevertheless the 'excuse' for the final break-up as far as Adrian was concerned. I also suspected that his antipathy towards 'us' was probably partly due to a characteristic of George that was OK in principle not in practice. He had the wishful hope that everything would work out all right for everyone in the end and, with this in mind, continued to write to Marjorie after he had left her. It didn't seem a good idea to me and presumably upset her, as a result of which Adrian - initially the one left still living at home - asked him to stop and thereafter only contacted his father when there was family business to discuss.

When I first saw him, I nearly burst out laughing. He looked so like the occasional photograph I'd seen of George when he was young and without a beard. Anyway, it was all very formal and civilised. His wife Karolyn seemed pleasant and of course the little girls were as sweet as little girls can be. We had coffee and it was agreed we should go out for a walk. Carol and Karolyn stayed at home with the girls. George and Adrian went on ahead, and Julian and

I caught up with each other's news. It was good to see, ahead of us, father and son engaged in the first one-to-one conversation for many a year.

Perhaps Julian read my thoughts. "I think I'll go back in case I can help," he said.

"I'll come with you," I said.

George overheard and said, "Mm I think I will, too." I'm not sure whether this was a masculine lack of insight or George being particularly obtuse.

"No you won't," I said. "It's ages since you and Adrian had a chance to catch up."

Julian and I turned back before he could argue.

It wasn't the most relaxed day I've ever had, but it was a lot better than it might have been. "What do you think?" George asked on the way home.

"You're very alike."

"Are we?" He sounded surprised.

"I mean to look at. I can't tell much more after such a short time." I thought a bit. "Perhaps a bit pompous, but that's probably the Civil Service influence."

"He says he wants to bring the family over during the summer."

They came over in August and we went for a local walk. Sally, the elder of the two children, clutched her grandfather's hand most of the time, and completely won him over.

----oOo----

Soon after our return, Prince Charles and Diana Princess of Wales had their second son Harry, though by most accounts the royal relationship was not ideal. On the other hand, Diana's involvement in several charities, not least for Aids sufferers, was widely applauded. After our Mississippi marathon, I thought we might lead a quieter life for a while. After all, we were respectively in our mid-fifties and sixties. But no.

"How about canoeing through Finland?" George ventured sometime in 1986. That was the year Claire and Mike decided to do a world tour, including six months in Australia.

"Finland's all lakes," I pointed out. "It can get windy on lakes. Not to mention confusing with those hundreds of islands."

But my caution didn't stand much chance as the Finns were on George's side, pointing out that many of the lakes were linked. We studied the map. The idea was that we would go by car, carrying the canoe on the roof.

"Look," George said pinpointing with a pencil. It was pointing at Enontekiö, about 300 miles north of the Arctic Circle. I had walked to it several times across the fells with Johanna from Pallastunuri. "We could put in to the Ounas river there and follow it all the way down to Rovaniemi on the Arctic Circle. Then we could pick up the car and drive to .... " The pencil hovered a while. ".... here and I reckon we could continue via connected lakes all the way to .... *here."* The pencil landed on Mikkeli which was indeed a long way south."

But first of all we had to get to Entontekiö. The Ounas river was potentially the most intriguing part of the trip for there were stretches of good current as well as the occasional need to portage and even more frequent need to line the canoe. The latter provided me with a long learning curve for it was the first time I had experienced this process - holding the canoe on a rope as we walked along the river bank. This was hard work as we often needed to manoeuvre round such obstacles as willow shrubs, or sections of rocky shore. We also had some good bird watching, especially the sight of an osprey both perching and in flight, on one occasion being mobbed by whimbrel. Otherwise it was pretty wet and cold for the next two or three days when we reached Kittilä. Another of our wild camps, it did at least give us the opportunity to do some walking during which we came across a youth hostel with a fine sauna of which we made good use.

Our first camp site beyond Kittilä rather unusually was beside an art museum. This was the home of the artist Reidar Säristöniemi who had died a few years earlier and had earned the reputation of being perhaps the best known artist in Lapland. The museum had been set up and was run by his brother. Reidar had been the son of a farming family, mainly breeding livestock including reindeer. His brother showed us round the gallery and in due course offered us coffee and eventually welcome accommodation in the dressing room next to the sauna by the river. Various new buildings were under construction including a pool, coffee shop and fishing pools, no doubt long since completed. The first guests to the gallery were arriving as we packed up to leave next morning.

There was, as usual, a northerly wind which at least came from behind us and initially helped us to take advantage of the quite brisk current so we made good time; then the river followed a protracted bend until we were almost facing into the wind, encouraging us to make an early camp. As we proceeded south and the river widened we noticed an increasing amount of floating timber. For a couple more days we alternated between slow and swift stretches, but we were also aware that ahead of us lay an extensive stretch of white water that it would not be wise for us to attempt to run with a laden open canoe. After a lot of discussion and bearing in mind we had much of the rest of Finland through which to canoe, George decided to go back north by bus to pick up the car to drive the last stretch back to Rovaniemi. It felt like cheating a bit, but we still had some hundreds of kilometres of lake canoeing to tackle, without the benefit of a current.

In fact, we managed to hit on the wettest summer Finland had had for forty years. Friends scattered about the country offered us hospitality, so we were to do quite a bit more 'cheating' for the weather continued to be dull, cold and often raining. We drove at leisure, sightseeing through Kuusamo, Kajaani and Iisalmi until we reached the northern stretches of Finland's massive central Saimaa lake district at Kuopio.

I was right to have reservations about canoeing through a large lake system, though I have to say that George was impressive in finding the right route with the aid of a compass and some guidance from the port and starboard markers of the lake traffic lanes. The light wind with which we started strengthened and, perversely, changed direction. Finding a camp site was also a challenge as this was a popular area for building summer houses; but when necessary I asked for permission in my stumbling Finnish and it was always granted. The weather did not improve. The wind stayed strong. Sometimes it was against us, when it could whip up the water into uncomfortable choppiness; sometimes it was behind us which could be helpful though, if it were really strong, I sometimes found myself paddling in mid-air, and for George steering from the rear it must have been quite a challenge. But finally the weather did improve and we enjoyed some pleasant paddling, camp sites and some good bird watching, including a couple of cranes on one occasion making the most of a field of hay.

Still it has to be said that one collection of islands surrounded by water is much like another. We had been offered hospitality by one or two friends who had a summer home on one of the lake islands and one of our stranger directions was to "look for an island with a red towel hanging outside the sauna." Miraculously we found it - or rather George did. There was a note congratulating us with instructions from the owners announcing they would be turning up the next day. They did, only to inform us after a few hours, during which we saw perhaps half a dozen small boats with outboard engines, that Finland was getting horribly overcrowded.

By now place names were beginning to sound familiar for we had both had earlier opportunities to travel parts of the Saimaa lake system by steamer. One of the places we were looking forward to revisit was Savonlinna, known for its opera festival and medieval castle. The latter is particularly satisfying, a classic example of what a medieval castle should look like, especially in western Europe. But as well as its own attractions Savonlinna is a good centre for visiting others. One of these is Punkaharju. 'Harju' means 'ridge' and Punkaharju is a particularly attractive one only 20 km. away from Savonlinna. It has long been a popular tourist destination, but more recently it had acquired a new highlight: a vast area of art galleries known as Retretti, much of it built out of living rock, set in landscaped grounds and the scene of changing art exhibitions each year. In contrast is the 19th century Kerimäki church, said to be the world's largest wooden church.

But undoubtedly our greatest treat was the performance of Carmen at the Opera Festival, by an Estonian company who were first class. It would have been hard to better the combination of the setting, the atmosphere and the singing.

We also visited the provincial museum which gave an excellent picture of the history of this important region, but also had a special display on the history of Saimaa's lake traffic in general and timber floating in particular. Lake traffic had begun in the 16th century and reached its heyday of 600 vessels in the 1920s and '30s. This was of great interest to us as the next day we were going to get close to the timber floating by spending a day on one of the tug boats that hauled one of these extremely long trains of bundled timber across the lakes.

Having been accustomed to tug boats on the Danube and push boats on the Mississippi, we found Saimaa's version of particular interest. 'Ours', the *Verna,* was positively tiny in comparison with those on our big rivers. In fact she was only 23 metres, but responsible for no less than 1560 bundles of timber, trailing behind her for over a kilometre and a half. And hauling timber across large expanses of water proved very different from manoeuvring barges along the narrow traffic lane of a big winding river. At times the tow boat had to find its way through narrow channels or a complexity of islands when it often lost sight of its 'cargo'. In those cases, especially as the light began to fade, the captain had to keep a weather eye on the line of lights which indicated the train of logs. It seemed he had to pay quite heavily for any bundles that were lost. Another essential part of the team was a smaller boat that chugged up and down the train of logs, nudging it here and there where necessary either to keep it in line or to assist it in manoeuvring a bend. On several occasions we passed a Russian vessel laden with logs. I wondered aloud why Finland needed to import logs from Russia. "They haven't much else to export," one of the crew said dryly.

Our time on the tug boat felt like luxury, and we left it with some reluctance. My diary records that we still had a further couple of weeks, partly paddling but mostly driving through the lake system, including a visit to Helsinki. And time and again my notes repeat the mantra '*and still it rains'*.. But there were lighter moments. After one such day of rain, we asked a farmer a few miles out of Mikkeli if there were a field where we could camp and he promptly offered us a shed for the night as well as use of the smoke sauna or *savusauna* they were lighting that evening.

The use of sauna in Finland goes back a couple of thousand years. The oldest known saunas were pits dug in a slope with heaped stones that were heated in one corner. Over time these developed into a four-cornered wooden hut with an earthen floor and a chimneyless stove, which served as both a primitive dwelling and a bath. While the stove was being heated the room filled with smoke which dispersed, leaving a distinct smoky smell. The old smoke sauna had come back into fashion, and was especially popular in the countryside.

I spent most of the remainder of our time in Finland checking material for my annual revision of Fodor Guides as well as enjoying the company of our friends Matti and Ritva. Finally they saw us off on the Silja Line ferry from Stockholm from which we drove to Gothenburg for the ferry back to Harwich. On the return drive home, we stopped at Cambridge to catch up with family news.

Though we could justifiably complain that we sometimes suffered from singular bad luck, especially when it came to weather, we had to admit that we were also prone to astonishingly good luck in other respects. One of these was to manifest itself soon after our return to England in August 1987. Claire and Mike had fairly recently returned from six months in Australia and their wedding was planned for the following month. For reasons I can't remember we had a guest staying with us just before the wedding date. He was a sort of climbing friend of George and was recovering from the major shock of having been left by his wife. Not surprisingly he was in a sorry state and made his way steadily through a bottle of Scotch. Just before his arrival, George had become aware of an uncomfortable health problem in that he was having increasing difficulty in being able to pee. The time between his disappearances to the loo became shorter and shorter and rather worrying. We managed to get our guest to bed, soon after which I telephoned the doctor on call. He bade me to put George in a warm bath and if that didn't work to ring him again.

It did not work and, with much appreciated alacrity, the doctor arrived on our doorstep, where he successfully if painfully administered to George affording him considerable relief, though we knew this could only be temporary. But when I thought of the isolated places through we had been travelling only a few weeks earlier I could not be thankful enough that we had made it home. We went to the surgery first thing in the morning where he was administered to again, and an urgent appointment made at the hospital. Here we saw a consultant who did some more administering and said that a very minor but necessary operation might involve a wait. Luckily (again!) a cancellation occurred and George was taken in straight away. He was insistent that I should still go to Claire's wedding, but I thought we had tested our luck far enough and that I was not going to risk being anywhere else until the operation was over. Instead I went to a Fellowship meeting, then visited him. By next day he was helping staff serve meals and the following one he was home.

In the meantime, Claire's and Mike's wedding was reported to have gone off very successfully and, having been much taken by Australia, the following year they emigrated there. They started off in Sydney but ended up in Perth, Western Australia where they both found employment. I could have a fair guess at what would happen before too long, and I wasn't wrong; within a few years their parents decided to follow suit.

With our long absence in Finland followed by preoccupation with Claire's wedding and George's unpredictable bladder, some world events had all but passed us by. In particular we had not fully registered the spreading and deep unease in the Middle East. Following the Six-Day war in 1967and Israel's annexation of the West Bank, there had been growing unrest and anger among the Palestinians at the increasing building of homes on the West Bank. But in addition to worryingly ongoing tensions between Israel and the Palestinians, there was a new cause for alarm.

Someone called Saddam Hussein had become a Big Cheese in Iraq This had become a kingdom under British control in 1920 and, eventually, after World War Two, a Ba'athist and then military republic under this ambitious general. He became renowned for the brutal control exercised over his predominantly Shia population. A few years later, neighbouring Iran rebelled against its autocratic Shah who was replaced by the exiled Ayatollah Khomeini and became a Shia Republic. Alarmed by the growing strength of his neighbour and using a border dispute as an excuse, Saddam Hussein invaded Iran in 1980 and in the course of an eight-year conflict many hundreds of thousands of deaths resulted, some as a result of chemical weapons used by Saddam Hussein on the Iranians and eventually his own people. Following Iraq's annexation of Kuwait in 1990, further conflict resulted in a further huge number of deaths. This proved to be only the beginning of unrest in the Middle East with devastating results, even discounting the ongoing Israel-Palestinian situation.

----oOo----

It was some time in the late eighties that Julian and Carol parted, and a while later that Julian remarried, this time Marilyn who had several children and grandchildren from her first marriage. Then, in due course I noticed that George seemed preoccupied, and was well aware that one of his foibles was to delay telling me anything potentially controversial until he could no longer avoid it. So, at last I said, "Well, are you going to tell me whatever you've been meaning to tell me?"

George prevaricated a while longer then said enigmatically, "It's that school in Somerset."

"Which school, and what about it?"

"Yes, well..." It seemed that a few months ago, Sue Someone, the head of a girls' boarding school where George lectured and who had also been a climbing friend, said she was thinking of taking their Sixth Form for a trek in Nepal. She had asked George if he would go as its leader. "And I said only if we had a doctor with us."

"And?"

"Well, she's just written to say that one of the girls has a doctor father who's willing to come. Jeremy Something."

"Hmmm. Where exactly are you going?"

"The general aim is Everest Base Camp, though I'm thinking of making it Kalar Pattarh which rises above it and gives great views of Everest." He put on what I called his 'spaniel look'. "So I wondered whether you would mind."

"When is it?"

"Over Christmas. This coming Christmas."

I allowed a small silence to lengthen before I said, "Oh, George..."

"I know it's a lot to ask. But it's a wonderful opportunity for the girls. And for me. In fact, apart from leaving you, I only have one reservation - the youngest girl is only fourteen. On the other hand, her father is a diplomat so even at that young age, Beth's already seen a considerable amount of the world."

I thought briefly of my fourteen-year-old self diving under the eiderdown as the ceiling descended on my head. Different eras, different experiences. Given the opportunity, would I have gone? Given my head for heights, probably not. But what a wonderful possibility for those who could.

George said encouragingly, "It won't be for that long."

"The girls will need enough time to acclimatise," I pointed out.

"They will. But it really is a wonderful opportunity," he repeated. "In fact, I'm sure you could come along too?" It was part of George's wishful thinking that he would try and talk me round with some unlikely possible reward. Gasping my way up to Everest Base Camp was not my idea of a fun way to spend Christmas, so I muttered a quick "No thanks." After a moment, George went on, "Well, if it's OK I thought it would be useful to meet this doctor, perhaps have him over for lunch?"

Yes, I'd rather like to meet him, too. "Good idea," I said.

When he came over one week-end in late April, Jeremy Something proved to be a lean, thoughtful man in his late fifties. Not a great deal earlier he had won Mastermind, which had alarmed George somewhat as they were sharing a tent. Fortunately he proved to be modest and sensible, too. That was a relief. It was good to know that there would be someone medical to keep an eye on George as well as the girls. Jeremy was a trekker rather than a climber which, perhaps foolishly, reassured me that this was should not to be too hazardous an adventure.

Over the coming weeks, both men gave Talks to the Girls, Jeremy on health issues, George on the culture and customs of the area and the need to respect the local people's attitude towards immodest dress. Jeremy talked to the girls as a group and individually. He assessed them as having unbounded enthusiasm and good health, with young Beth as fit as any of them. In addition to the two men there were to be two teachers.

It was while George was away on a series of talks that Adrian rang. I blurted out his plans without thinking. There was a disapproving mutter before Adrian said, "Typical. He always was a self-centred ...."

I had come to understand over time that he was the one who had most resented George's absences during their childhood, and no doubt his departure to live with me. I wondered if any of the sons realised the impact the war had had on their father with the loss of so many friends, the major air accident, fractured skull, long p.o.w. stay, all happening so soon after his school days. Probably not. Now Adrian paused "So what will you do for Christmas?"

"Go to my sister's," I said off the top of my head, and then thought what a good idea that was. In fact it would only be my second visit to Wiltshire since Sinette and Len moved to Marlborough the previous year. And I'd be able to catch up on news of Nick and Claire, now both well established in Australia in the New Year, and any plans their parents had for emigration. I decided not to tell George of Adrian's call.

Things worked out a good deal better than I anticipated. George was picked up ten days before Christmas by a minibus packed with the school group and all their paraphernalia. Several neighbours came out to see them off and there was quite a festive air, leaving me somewhat deflated when the minibus finally turned the corner and was out of sight. Still I wasn't allowed much time for moping. One neighbour invited me for supper that evening, two others for drinks parties the following week. Then there were things to get ready for Marlborough, articles to finish, last-minute presents to buy. In all, it was a busy time, but a couple of days before Christmas I was glad to load the car and head for Marlborough. It was a long time since I'd spent any length of time with Sinette and Len, and it was good to catch up on their and the children's news.

It was also a long time since I'd had the sort of Christmas that had marked our childhood even through the war. The focal point of this was the Christmas tree, pre-and post war sent out by my favourite Swiss aunt, during the war rather makeshift. We had also kept up the tradition of decorating the tree the Swiss way with live candles. This had driven Dad and subsequently George, other relatives and (usually male) friends to distraction, with constant and tiresome comments about warning the fire brigade. I learned to live with, then ignore these. To this tradition I'd added my own: what I called my international population – small figures or other items from different parts of the world, either fixed to the branches or tucked in among a carpet of spruce branches under the tree. During my travels over the years, I'd collected a couple of very small koala bears from Australia, a reindeer from Finland, an old man from Poland, church bells from Nepal, and a camel from Egypt.

Interestingly Adrian's children equally came to love the candlelight tradition we'd developed of guessing which of the lit candles would be the last to go out. The other challenge for the grandchildren would be to guess the origins of the 'population'.

On Christmas morning we went for a walk on the Wiltshire downs. Lunch was late but magnificent. Sinette had always been a marvellous cook and, by the time we'd finished and loaded the dishwasher, we all declared themselves 'stuffed' and collapsed in front of the television to watch the Queen's speech and fall asleep, not necessarily in that order. Then it was time for the candles to be lit, and it was during the candle-lit time, Christmas music playing quietly in the background, that I had one of the worst aching moments of missing George.

Later I learned that six thousand miles away, George was having one of those aching missing moments, too. Overall it had been an immensely successful trip. The girls had mostly adapted magnificently, with only a few worrying incidents of altitude sickness. Jeremy was a tower of strength with his knowledge and his reassurance. His decision to bring 14-year-old Beth had been completely justified. In fact, she was coping with the rough conditions, long days and, not least, altitude, rather better than most. Of course in many respects, the girls had an 'easy' time. The Sherpas carried all the luggage, went on ahead to make camp, erect the tents and prepare for the next meal. They awoke the girls between 6-7 a.m. with a cheery "Good morning, Sir, tea?" which amused them no end. It took them a while to wake up properly, so breakfast was a leisurely affair. The walking day, however, was quite demanding and they were on the move for several hours before they stopped for lunch.

Several had had rather nasty bouts of altitude sickness and been sent back to lower altitudes with one or two Sherpas. By the time they reached Nanche Bazaar, the Sherpa 'capital', about a third of the party had turned back and several more decided to stay in Nanche Bazaar.

By then the group had further dwindled. George reported that it seemed a bit hard on Beth as she was one of only two school girls left along with the headmistress and sports teacher, and soon after that the other girl and teachers had to be sent back. Beth, with a maturity gained no doubt from her considerable travels, proved to be good company and George was determined she would reach their final goal in as relaxed a state as possible. So finally they stood, George, Beth and a guide, on the summit of Kalar Pattarh looking across at the rugged triangle of Everest's summit framed between closer tops.

The whole venture made a huge impression on Beth and later she came to share it with us. By then she had grown up, married and had her first child and we were touched that she wanted to keep the friendship alive across the generations. Indeed one of the aspects she remembered as most important was the bond with George and her friendship with the Sherpas. There were more humorous memories, too, such as being awoken at 6 a.m. by the Sherpas' cheery awakening. Without going into detail, she remembered a yak dung fight and a dog that followed her for two days. Less pleasant were the headaches from washing hair in a glacial river.

She also remembered the magnificent monastery at Thyangboche where she had walked round the prayer wheels that were an intrinsic part of a Buddhist temple, spinning the wheels and murmuring as she went from one to another, *please let me get to the top, please let me get to the top.* I remembered that George had been especially pleased to note her interest in local culture.

A few weeks later, I sat in the cafeteria at Paddington Station and glanced at my watch for the umpteenth time. Five minutes to go, and I wanted to be there first. I gathered up my bag and copy of a newspaper, smiling as I remembered the first time I had experienced a similar circumstance. Then it had been our first meeting in Tottenham Court Road; now it was by the Paddington Station clock and I had been there a couple of minutes when a familiar voice said, "Darling!", and the next second I was enjoying the kind of hug I had not had for a very long time.

----oOo----

A couple more significant things happened as we entered the last decade of the 20th century. The first was that Julian, having separated from Carol, became remarried to Marilyn. The second was that my depression had become particularly tiresome and, having discussed this with my sponsor in the Fellowship, I decided to follow her advice and for the first time consult a counsellor. He was called Oliver, lived just outside Oxford and initially I made the grave mistake of thinking he would tell me what to do. Not at all. There were long silences while he waited for me to tell him what the problem was at which point he would prod me into considering various options.

"Of course," I told him at last, "the depression is all my fault."

Oliver looked interested. "Is this what you have been told?"

No it wasn't. It was just something I had assumed as I had assumed most of the more negative aspects of my life were my fault. So, I gradually learned that this was one of the symptoms of depression, that it could be easier to stay at the bottom of a dark hole than face the struggle up into the light. With Oliver's help I chose the latter path

It wasn't cheap but I stopped smoking at the same time which more or less paid for our sessions. So I suppose I had a double benefit. After about a year, Oliver said he thought we had done all we could unless I wanted to go deeper into my childhood psyche. I didn't, so we agreed to stop the sessions. I am still grateful to him all these years later. And though the depression did not disappear forever, I gradually learned new techniques for dealing with it.

1990s: house move

It's weird how everything often seems to happen at once. A house move had been high on the 'to do' list for some time: in fact since they had changed the flight path of the F111s at RAF Upper Heyford. It was decided that because these aircraft were no longer as young as they used to be, the need for them to do a sharp turn to avoid overflying our village now held an element of risk and it was decreed they should continue straight over our heads.

Given the reason for this change, it did not leave those of us living under the new flight path with a feeling of great confidence. And the noise was horrendous. From my office window I could see them take off and they rarely did it singly. Once they started I could put off making any further telephone calls for a half-hour or so, and we wouldn't dream of sitting out in the garden. Anyway the house really was too small and we had long been thinking we needed more space. The use of the dining room as George's office was far from ideal when we had visitors, and catering for the latter overnight was a problem. The need to move suddenly seemed more urgent.

The other priority was to decide where we wanted to move. We both liked the idea of Deddington, only five miles away to the north, as we did some of our shopping there, our health centre was also there and, finally, around Christmas 1991, an appropriate house came on the market. In addition to the village's varied facilities, the house had extra rooms so we would each have an office as well as a proper spare room for visitors. Nita, the owner of our prospective new home, seemed quite surprised to have viewers in the middle of the Festive season. We took to her, and also felt a great deal of sympathy for apparently her husband had dropped dead in the middle of doing crossword on the rail journey home from London. Anyway, we were taken by the house and said we would be back with an offer very shortly.

It was at about this time that Sinette and Len finally decided to emigrate to Australia and, though I regretted it, it was no great surprise. Nick had gone to live there in 1982, and Claire and Mike in

1988, so it did not take rocket science to forecast that their parents would follow in due course. I felt a bit wan about it. Now they made definitive plans and it worked out that they would emigrate about a month after our move, probably spending their last few nights in the UK with us. It was a few weeks after the Maastricht Treaty created the European Union.

By the time Sinette and Len came, we were more or less straight, except for the stacks of boxes of books in the hall and any other spare corner. It was both lovely and sad having them there for those few days and, both being practical, they helped us with jobs about the house and garden. But I didn't go and see them off at the airport as this was a farewell that didn't have a foreseeable end. As the car disappeared round the corner, I felt weirdly as though I were the last person left standing.

----oOo----

While we were busy reviewing future accommodation, it seemed a good time to review other aspects of my life, in particular where I was going - if anywhere - in the book-writing field. My efforts to interest either publisher or agent in a book on our canoe journey down the Mississippi had had dismal results. Several found the theme simply fascinating, but there was always a 'but ... *but* ... **but'** and it had become very tedious. It did not help that an award-winning travel writer had recently produced a highly successful book on the same theme: the main difference was that Jonathan Raban had had an engine and a two-way radio - though he was admittedly alone - on the descent of the Mississippi he described in his *Old Glory.* George had tried to discourage me from reading it before we left on our own venture, afraid that it would put me off. In fact, Mr. Raban might have been travelling on a totally different river - and on the whole I preferred ours.

On the other hand, technology had been developing at an amazing pace, I had joined the digital world and was tolerably competent at word processing. I began to look into and to think seriously about self-publishing. Research led me to Antony Rowe Ltd. who specialised in short print runs and I made contact with a lass called Tanya, who sounded and was Russian and very efficient, if tending to be a little bossy and over-optimistic on how much could be achieved in a given time. She knew about computers, too, and saved me a lot of effort in avoiding the worst page lay-out blips. She was also quite persuasive and I'm still not sure how many of the decisions made were hers rather than mine. The costs did seem reasonable though it meant making compromises, notably abandoning the idea of including photographs in order to keep costs down. Sinette thought of the title. While I sought something clever, I happened to mention that locally the Mississippi was known as the Big Muddy.

"That'd make a great title," my sister pointed out, and so it stuck. At this time self-publishing, then sometimes unflatteringly referred to as vanity publishing, was just beginning to gain some respectability. It was far from acquiring the highly sophisticated procedures of the future, and still clung to some of the hang-ups of traditional printing - in particular the pricing was largely governed by the number of copies printed, so that the more you printed, the cheaper per copy the book would be. This mattered less if you were a commercial operation, unless you were an individual in charge of writing, promoting, printing, storing and selling - especially if you were an individual in the process of moving house.

In the end, I (or was it Tanya?) settled on 1500 copies. At that stage, in order to keep costs down, I decided to avoid illustrating it with photographs; instead George's great friend Tom Price designed the cover and produced some line drawings as chapter headings. I'm not sure this was the best decision, but it seemed right at the time. It was quite a small book, and 1500 didn't sound so very many until they arrived in a considerable number of boxes to be stored away in various wardrobes or built-in cupboards.

One of the reasons for going ahead with publication, despite the move, was that a few weeks later the International Canoe Exhibition was taking place at Crystal Palace and this seemed an ideal venue at which to launch my baby. I'm not sure what I expected but ninety-something sales did not strike me as anything but disappointing, but then in retrospect from the early 21st century, I can look back with wry amusement at my innocence in relation to the promotion and sale of books. In fact, my sales were quite good - it was merely that my expectations were too high in this as in many other things. Publicity in the local press was helpful and in those days, before all bookshops belonged to a handful of companies, the local bookshop did me proud.

One of the first people in Deddington to become a close friend was Marianne Elsley. Marianne was Jewish and had been sent over to England on the *kindertransport* early in 1939 when it became obvious that Germany was no longer the ideal place for a Jewish teenager to be brought up. She had been fostered here by a Quaker family, trained to become a nurse, met and married Ralph Elsley a British Gentile, become matron in a British public school and, in retirement, heavily engaged in British village life, even editing the *Deddington News* for a substantial period. I first encountered her at a meeting in the village where she was giving a talk on her childhood in Germany and upbringing in Britain. She was a natural speaker and the talk was moving in the extreme in its understatement of what she - and especially her parents - had gone through.

One of the most touching of her stories was when Jewish families were forbidden to keep domestic pets, and Marianne had opened the window of the flat and put before it the cage containing her pet canaries, letting them free over the streets of Berlin. It is doubtful that they survived long. Marianne's parents had left their own departure too long and perished in Auschwitz. I was anxious that George should meet her as soon as possible and we invited her and Ralph round for the evening. As I thought we had a lot in common and we became good friends.

It was also through Marianne that I became involved in the Deddington Writers' Group - or indeed that the group came into existence. Marianne and another local writer, Molly Neild, met from time to time to discuss writing. And then out of the blue a newcomer to the village, Kristin Thomson, put a letter in the D.N. enquiring whether there was a meeting for writers. As a result we got together and decided that this would be a good idea. We met once a month in one of our homes with the idea of discussing a contribution from two of our group; this contribution had to be circulated among the other group members in advance of the meeting so we had time to read it. This was made so much easier by the provenance of computers and now email to which we all subscribed. We also decided that, between meetings, we would try and sell stories or articles to established markets and report any successes (or failures). Some of us were more assiduous than others at doing this, but it did keep us on our toes.

Early on we had also befriended the then current editors of the *Deddington News,* Norman Stone and his wife Angela. They had been editing it for about seven years and had been trying for some time, without success, to shed this responsibility. Both were retired Civil Servants and Norman had written several books on public relations, as well as having been heavily involved with decimalisation. Having tried unsuccessfully to find a successor for some time, Norman announced firmly that he planned to hold a meeting of all those interested in keeping the magazine in existence and unless someone came forward, it would cease to exist. As he intended, this concentrated everyone's mind very effectively.

The general consensus was that it should continue and a date was set for a meeting. Norman presided over it, suggesting that we should create a team and this or that person should take charge of this or that section of the magazine. It seemed as though I was faring rather well out of this as Norman delegated various areas of responsibilities: features, church and chapel, parish council meetings, letters to editor, etc. But when I voiced this thought, he simply grinned and said, "Oh I've put you down as managing editor!"

As already mentioned, like a lot of people, I had taken the first steps towards upgrading my means of communication, progressing from a typewriter to something called an Amstrad. Amstrad was founded in 1968 by Alan Sugar at the age of 21, the name of the original company being AMS Trading (Amstrad) Limited, derived from its founder's initials (Alan Michael Sugar). Amstrad entered the market in the field of consumer electronics. During the 1970s they were at the forefront of low-priced hi-fi, TV and car stereo cassette technologies. In 1985, the popular Amstrad PCW range was introduced, which were principally word processors, complete with printer, running the Locoscript word processing programme. By means of floppy discs, text could be transferred from one Amstrad to another and as several members of the DN team had acquired one it was, of course, immensely time-saving when it came to editing. In due course I graduated further to a laptop computer; it was on 'special offer' at £1500, which a few years later would have been considered exorbitant at half the price. The digital age had arrived

Norman joined our writing group as did another man in the village, bringing our membership to six. We were an interesting cross-section. Marianne had specialised in writing of her experiences as a refugee; Molly had written quite a lot for children and also about Africa where she and her husband John had spent most of their married life; Norman favoured the unusual and, occasionally, outrageous; the other man specialised in cars; Kristin was by far the most academic and regularly caused us to use a dictionary; I was probably the only one who regarded writing as a means of earning money.

----oOo----

The 1990s saw a good deal more strife as well as some re-writing of the world map. The strife continued in Israel/Palestine, exacerbated by the Oslo Accords by which Israel affirmed actions they did not follow through. The re-writing of the map, alas, was due to the break-up of one of my favourite countries, Yugoslavia. Its growing unrest had been in the news for some time and gradually it began topping the headlines. I've already described how the dismantling of the Ottoman empire after the First World War re-arranged the map of the Middle East, creating borders that were to trigger appalling hatreds and strife decades later. Likewise the Habsburg empire was divided up into several parts (Hungary, First Austria Republic, Kingdom of Yugoslavia, First Czechoslovak Republic, Second Polish Republic, Kingdom of Romania, most of which were subsequently renamed). Since the border between Habsburg and Ottoman had run through the middle of Yugoslavia for several hundred years, the scene was set for conflict.

In the 7th century AD, Islam was born and within a century its empire spread from Iberia in the west to the Indus river in the east, giving rise to a civilisation that was noted especially for its astronomers, mathematicians, doctors and philosophers, as well as the high rate of literacy among its population. Like Judaism and Christianity, Islam followed the monotheistic principles of the Bible, and initially there was a good deal of tolerance between the three faiths, all founded on the same original scriptures and in the same part of the Middle East. Alas it was not to last.

In the meantime, Ottoman Turkey was founded at the end of the 13th century by Osman the First and became the seat of the Ottoman Empire which, within a century, had extended across the Balkans, eventually to the gates of Vienna. It thus established itself as the caliphate, i.e. the territory ruled by the Caliph or spiritual leader of Islam regarded by many to be the successor to Mohammed. The Ottoman Caliphate was abolished by Ataturk in 1924. Rightly or wrongly, I judged the caliphate to be the Islamic version of Rome.

In the Middle Ages there followed the often bloody history of the Crusades, not the prettiest episode of the Christian story. Later still Europe itself came under different growing power centres, one of which was Vienna seat of the strengthening Habsburg empire. So, eventually, Habsburg and Ottoman faced each other across the great divide that ran more or less directly north to south through the middle of Yugoslavia. And its divisions were not only political but alphabetic (west Latin, east Cyrillic) and religious (west Roman Catholic, east Islamic and Orthodox). Thus it remained, more or less, until both Habsburg and Ottoman were defeated in World War One.

Within the Kingdom of Yugoslavia, the two main ethnic groups - the Serbs on the Ottoman side, the Croats on the Habsburg side, each strengthened their cultural importance and political ambitions. The new nation did not get off to an easy start, nor was the situation helped by the rumblings that forecast the Second World War. During the latter a Fascist state was set up in Croatia by the right wing Ustaše and, during its reign, hundreds of thousands of Serbs were slaughtered in concentration camps. In the meantime Tito led his Partisans and their supporters into a guerrilla war against the Germans and post-war became President of the new Federal Republic of Yugoslavia made up of six self-governing republics: Slovenia, Croatia, Serbia, Bosnia-Herzegovina, Macedonia and Montenegro. But Serbs and Croats never overcame their deep antipathy towards each other, nourished by their ethnic pride and centuries of living apart.

Under Tito, the new young Communist state did rather well, establishing its independence from the Russian-influenced Warsaw Pact countries and, thereby earning the economic support of the West. Inevitably there were marked differences in the progress of the individual self-determining republics. Slovenia and Croatia, with their more developed motivation drawn from centuries of Habsburg influence, prospered rather more rapidly than Bosnia, Macedonia and Montenegro. Serbia, which had once dominated its own small medieval empire, was impatient for independence, active in its ambition to pursue its development free from Ottoman influence and restrictions.

The several republics which made up the Yugoslav Federation began to show growing unrest and desire for independence. Slovenia, the most prosperous of the six republics, was the first to declare this in 1991. It was followed by Croatia in the same year and, given the historic rivalry between Croatia and Serbia, this was a much greater trigger for strife. Though internationally Serbia was held to blame for much of the bloodshed, appalling acts were committed by both sides, as also in the civil war that split Bosnia-Herzegovina in two. A high number of Serbs had lived in Croatia for hundreds of years, in particular along the old 'Habsburg border' with the Ottoman Empire. They were quickly disenfranchised and left in droves for an uncertain future in Serbia and no doubt conscious of the treatment received by many Serbs from the Croats during the Second World War.

In neighbouring Bosnia-Herzegovina the situation was in some ways much worse, for here Roman Catholic Croats, Orthodox Serbs and Moslem Bosniaks had lived and intermarried quite peaceably for a long time. My good Bosnian Serb friends were quite accustomed to leave the keys to their home in the charge of their Bosniak neighbours and until quite late on would not believe that Civil War could become a reality. But it could and did.

I remember that the brother of my Bosnian Serb friend was rather active in Serbian politics and tried to persuade his brother to join him. My friend apparently protested, "But I have spent my life trying to understand the other person's point of view. Why should I become a politician?!"

Bosnia-Herzegovina showed increasing signs of Islamic influence and when it declared its independence, it received much practical support from those in the Middle East with an axe to grind. Yugoslavia's (by now mainly Serb) army made every attempt to prevent it. Not least, the army became entrenched in the hills surrounding Sarajevo subjecting the city to many months of siege in which a considerable number of its citizens died. Finally, the fate was sealed of what was to become the former Yugoslavia - i.e. turning it from one federated republic into six separate ones.

Also in the nineties and at the other end of the continent, Europe acquired three other new countries. That was on 6th September 1991 when Russia recognised the independence of the three Baltic states of Latvia, Lithuania and Estonia. I could guess what was coming before George said, "Three new countries to visit." I had paid a there-and-back day visit to the Estonian capital of Tallinn from Helsinki a few years earlier. The two countries had close cultural ties.

We had recently bought a new campervan - a slightly less old version of the VW - and, in 1993, decided to go the whole hog: covering most of Poland before crossing into the Baltic States, Russia and then into Finland. And we had a couple of rather important missions to fulfill along the way. George wanted to visit Stalag Luft III, one of the p.o.w. camps in which he had been held but better known as the scene of some daring escapes for which there had been cruel retributions. The other was to meet the request of our dear Jewish friend Marianne Elseley in Deddington, whose parents had perished in Auschwitz. She had never found the courage to visit the concentration camp and who could blame her. When she heard we were going, she asked if we would put some flowers somewhere in the camp in memory of her parents. Of course we agreed.

The trip needed a lot of organisation, not least obtaining letters of introduction for the Baltic States which were only just establishing some kind of tourist information facilities. We travelled across the North Sea from Harwich to Hamburg and, and after an overnight camp, crossed into Poland. Our first goal was Zagan, site of Stalag Luft III p.o.w. camp. As anyone who has followed World War II history, or seen the film *The Great Escape*, after weeks of tunnelling seventy-six prisoners escaped from this reputedly impregnable place, of whom seventy-three were recaptured. Later the Germans discovered that the operation had involved the use of 4,000 bed boards, ninety double bunk beds, 635 mattresses. amongst much else. The event also became known for the harsh reprisals in which fifty prisoners were shot. Most of the camp had gone, but the forests were still there together with the railway station where George must have disembarked over sixty years earlier, and a memorial to prisoners who were shot.

When we first decided to visit Krakow and Auschwitz, I told George I couldn't face going into the camp, now a museum. I'd read enough about the Holocaust to know what happened there and it didn't seem necessary to reinforce the pictures in my head. Having promised Marianne we would leave flowers in memory of her mother, I changed my mind. At least that was something I could do for her. First we visited Krakow itself, 68 km away on the Vistula river, Poland's second largest city, one of its oldest and a major cultural and economic centre.

Then we headed for Auschwitz. It was impressive that now, half a century after the end of the war, so many visitors still came. We bought flowers - where to put them was another matter, but we decided on a place where many people had been shot and where many flowers already had been placed. One bunch bore a simple message of sorrow from a British coach driver. In addition to the flowers I placed candles in several places in memory of Marianne's parents, mostly in the vicinity of the remains of several gas chambers.

Altogether there was a network of camps and sub camps, expanding as the Nazi conquered more of Europe. The network, covering an area of about 40 square kilometres and incorporating Auschwitz I and Auschwitz II-Birkenau, became closed to the outside world. In particular, Birkenau was where ethnic cleansing was carried out on an industrial scale. In many cases, victims arrived by train direct to the gas chambers. Of the others, most would have been segregated on arrival: the weak from the strong, the unhealthy from the healthy, the old and very young from those who still had some slave labour left in them. The weak went straight to the gas chambers. It was impossible to visualise the scenes of unimaginable partings that took place within sight of where we were standing. Between one and one-and-a-half million victims perished here. For those who were allowed to survive conditions were appalling and many died from lack of food or overwork.

We walked around these desolate places almost in silence. To break the quiet with the sound of voices almost seemed an insult. We had been told that you would not even hear birdsong here, but time must have done some healing for, as we approached groves of trees planted to disguise the ruins of the crematoria, we heard one of our favourites, the high fluting call of a golden oriole.

It was rather a relief to leave this area and head for the Tatras mountains bordering Slovakia. The weather wasn't brilliant but there was a wholesomeness about the rugged scenery which helped to cleanse memory. After a few days we reached Warsaw and the remarkable reconstruction of its Old Town following its 80% destruction by German forces. In the process of reconstruction the same stones were used and special kilns created to make the bricks to preserve its authenticity. It is a remarkable achievement even if purists will be able to notice differences from the original as shown in old paintings and prints.

And so, finally, to Lithuania. As we approached it we began to hear hair-raising stories of the length of time it took to cross the border. Forty-eight hours seemed to be the most common estimate. Presumably the novelty of being able to cross into these newly independent Baltic states had not yet worn off - not to mention the economic possibilities of black market trading such as the disposition of cars that had somehow found their way into Poland from Western Europe. When we finally reached the end of the queue at the border, we found we were twenty kilometres from the frontier. George fumed quietly, then not so quietly. Most people seemed content to settle down for the long wait. From time to time a vehicle or two drove passed us, one assumed with special dispensation though, judging from the reactions of others in the queue, this was not universally recognised. From time to time a heavy truck would drive into the left lane to block them and there would be noisy altercations. In the first four hours we crept forward a couple of kilometres.

Somehow a further eight hours passed: dozing, fretting, having a meal, drinking coffee. Finally encouraged by a Latvian truck driver, George suddenly said, "Let's go," and drove forward.

For a short while nobody seemed to notice our temerity, then a heavy truck began to pull forward to block us, noticed our GB plate, and apparently thought better of it. We seemed to be driving for ages, then our consciences got the better of us and George found a place to draw in. Someone indicated that the frontier really was not far ahead. George wandered off to investigate and returned visibly enthusiastic.

"I showed them our letter of introduction," he said. "They said we can go."

We tried to do it as surreptitiously as possible and, if there were protests, we managed to ignore them. Within a few minutes we had crossed the border into Lithuania, a country new to both of us, though naturally it did not look all that different.

For their rather small size, the three Baltic states have a lot of history, much of it linked or tied up with that of Poland, Germany and Russia. But perhaps the most rousing event was then within living memory of many of us: on 23rd August, 1989 approximately two million people across the three Baltic states formed a human chain spanning 675.5 kilometres (419.7 miles), hands joined and holding candles and national flags. The amount of organisation must have been phenomenal to ensure the chain was not broken. Indeed it was necessary in many cases to transport participants by bus to maintain the continuity. This remarkable achievement became known as the Baltic Chain or Chain of Freedom, and it was held on what was to mark the 50th anniversary of so-called Black Ribbon Day, the day that Molotov and Ribbentrop signed the pact between the Soviet Union and Nazi Germany dividing eastern Europe into spheres of influence which led to occupation of the Baltic states by Russia in 1940. Black Ribbon Day also became known as Remembrance Day for the victims of Stalinism and Nazism.

So, now we headed towards the capital Vilnius, stopping on the way at the small town of Druskininkai where we were blessed by one of those pieces of good fortune that often punctuates unplanned travel. Having stopped to ask a group if anyone spoke English, one of them said 'we all do' - it was a teacher with his pupils whom he was taking to meet a group of Americans. They led us to a small restaurant which also had accommodation where we had the best night for a long time.

The Lithuanian countryside was pleasant rather than dramatic - rolling farmland interspersed with forests. A characteristic we soon became aware of was represented by the many wood carvings known as *Rupintojelis*. This can be translated as combined anxiety, concern and solicitude and is a regular subject in Lithuanian woodcarving: depicting a man in a sitting position, looking pensively and sadly at passers-by. It can be found in the home, at crossroads and other public places.

In the Lithuanian capital, Vilnius, we found the helpful office of Lithuanian Tourist who plied us with coffee and information. We followed their advice and headed for a campsite about 25 km away on the road to Minsk where we rented a room for a couple of nights. Next day we had a morning of sightseeing back in Vilnius. The old part was delightful and the cathedral was in process of renovation in readiness for a visit from the Pope a few weeks later. We also learned quite a lot about the local mafia and the preponderance of cars with foreign number plates which had found their way here. The foreign number plates have to be replaced within a year, so those we saw represented only the tip of the iceberg.

In all we spent about a week in Lithuania, roaming the countryside as we made our way towards the Baltic in pursuit of George's quest to find one of the p.o.w. camps where he was kept for a short while during the war. This brought us close to the border with Kaliningrad, that curious small enclave of Russia sandwiched between Lithuania and Poland. George's camp had been near the town of Šiluté. As soon as we mentioned it, someone pointed us towards the local *Biblioteka* where the librarian seemed immediately to know what we sought, made us some coffee and telephoned for a local journalist who drove us at breakneck speed to the site. There was not much left for George to identify. The place had subsequently been used as a Soviet concentration camp in which innumerable Lithuanians had perished, and any graves were simply unidentifiable mounds. It was a forlorn place.

It was time to head into Latvia. This time the frontier was just a long straight road, so straight - according to my notes - that you could see into tomorrow, and we had no problems and no delays. Some New Zealanders in Lithuania had told of us a camp site so we aimed for that but clearly found the wrong one as it was quite appalling, but its situation by a lake and in pine woods was lovely so we made the best of a bad job. You needed to do that quite a lot with our kind of travel. Next day there was a hair raising drive into the capital Riga - during which we decided that the Lithuanians and Latvians were in competition with each other for earning the title of being the worst drivers in Europe; or perhaps just then the novelty of independence had gone to their heads.

We found Riga charming with its narrow streets and variety of old architecture much of it still in need of renovation. In contrast was the art nouveau of so many of its buildings. The city also offered an unexpected pleasure in the form of buskers - single, in pairs or in one case a trio, nearly all of them playing classical music, reflecting the city's long musical tradition, especially in opera and ballet. It was in Riga, too, we had our first haircuts in a long time, costing about a quarter of the price it would at home.

The enormous Bay of Riga which, from all accounts, is bordered by a mega sandy beach seemed inaccessible by road when we were there and we had a rather fruitless day driving round it without seeing it. Indeed our experience of Latvia was of forests and more forests, so we decided to leave a little earlier for neighbouring Estonia which I knew had close cultural affinities with Finland on the opposite side of the Gulf of Finland.

Our next border crossing brought a new problem. There didn't seem to be any traffic queues, but on the other hand nothing much seemed to be happening. We got talking to some Dutch travellers also waiting and after a couple of hours decided that was long enough. George and two of the Dutch made a foray to the border and asked to speak to someone in charge. This took some further time to be discussed and at last they were told that the officer could only speak to one of them at a time, and that behind closed doors. George went into the office, the door closed behind him. He was not there long. Quite soon he came out looking explosive to tell us that we could go through straight away for the payment of $40 per car.

Having told the officer that in our country such behaviour would have earned him a prison sentence, it was clearly deemed that we needed to cool our heels longer - four-and-a-half hours I think it was. We reminded ourselves of the Estonians' spunkiness in singing their way to freedom and decided to make allowance for one immigration officer. The Singing Revolution had been a development from the Baltic Chain we had first heard of in Lithuania. The year following that event, on 11 September 1988, a massive song festival, called "Song of Estonia", was held at the Tallinn Song Festival Arena. Nearly 300,000 people came together, more than a quarter of all Estonians, to express their ambition to regain independence. The Singing Revolution in Estonia lasted, with various protests and acts of defiance, until 1991. In that year, as Soviet tanks attempted to stop the progress towards independence, the Estonian Supreme Soviet together with the Congress of Estonia proclaimed the restoration of the independent state of Estonia and repudiated Soviet legislation. People acted as human shields to protect radio and TV stations from the Soviet tanks. Through these actions Estonia regained its independence without any bloodshed. All the same we reported the $40 incident to the Embassy on our return home and were told that the officer concerned had been dealt with; we hoped guiltily this did not mean he had been shot at dawn.

At last we were able to cross into Estonia and the changes were almost immediately obvious. The farmland was better tended, as were the small communities through which we passed. Now there were plenty of signs to tell us where we were and to point us to hotels and campsites. Because of its linguistic and cultural affinities with Finland, I immediately felt at home. When we reached the campsite at Estonia's capital, Tallinn, it had a restaurant though no means of changing money which was immediately overcome by the pleasant girl in charge who lent us the money.

Tallinn is a beautiful city. We called in at Estonian Travel first, where we were given some good information and conflicting advice about crossing into Russia. The advice ranged from the border being completely closed because of construction work to being open for tourists. We decided to check again in a few days and, in the meantime, accept whatever came along. All the same, the uncertainty brought on an attack of my old anxiety until George pointed out that if the worst came to the worst we could always miss Russia out and cross to Helsinki by sea. We spent a lot of the first day wandering around Tallinn. The degree of private enterprise was noticeable - in addition to established stalls individual women were selling fresh strawberries, bilberries and raspberries and, later in the day, hand-knitted sweaters. Friends of Finnish friends met us for lunch and told us more about the second hand car business; earlier Finns and Swedes had sold their own cars second hand, but now the competition from the 'availability' of western cars had curbed that source of income.

We headed first for south Estonia, via +Estonia's historic second city of Tartu   Amusingly, as we stopped to take photographs on the outskirts of town, we were accosted by a young man who switched to English when he heard our nationality. "Please could you tell me the way to Russia?" he asked. "I don't have a map." Not a road direction we were likely to get again in a hurry; apparently he was trying to get back to Siberia but we didn't feel it appropriate to ask why. On the question of maps, on enquiry at bookshops here and in Tallinn, we found we could get one of almost anywhere in the world except St. Petersburg which we needed and which lay just over the horizon. A little further, on our way to the hilly district of Otepää, we were stopped by the traffic police for speeding. This was in a small community where the speed limit applied to a short distance of a few hundred metres and we noticed that there seemed to be a steady clientele at the local open air restaurant waiting to be entertained by the police halting unsuspecting cars.

Otepää is a small town known as Estonia's winter capital because of its ski slopes, but it also has summer attractions including a small community on the sandy shore of Puhajarv lake where we stayed a couple of nights in a pleasant rural retreat in the form of wooden chalets. The next day we toured the area and gave ourselves the satisfaction of going to the top of the highest point not only of Estonia, but apparently of the three Baltic states: Suur Munamägi, all of 1043 feet (318 metres).

We had two more nights in Tallinn and learned that there were no problems for private vehicles travelling into Russia so decided to resume our journey. And, indeed, we crossed the border with absolutely no delays at all.

I have only been in Russia three times, but on each occasion have felt a touch uneasy. Perhaps it's because the norms of what are considered right and wrong don't quite match up to the realities. There are probably few more societies that are more controlled, yet also few where illegal actions are more rife.

Our first task, however, was to find the campsite which we had selected on a visit to Intourist, the Russian travel office before leaving London. Indeed the business of finding anything proved to have both its humorous and puzzling aspects. The fact is that I can - with difficulty - read the Cyrillic alphabet, though rather like a small child who has just learned to read, mouthing the letters until they form a word. This is not a quick way of reading street names and finding your way round a city. So George drove while I mouthed away and tried to keep an eye open for traffic whose discipline was questionable and whose trams were numerous and unpredictable.

When we eventually became irrevocably lost, we stopped at a small hotel where helpful girls did their best to point us in the right direction, which they deemed to be northwards on the way to Vyborg. At one point our spirits rose as the name of the campsite actually appeared on a roadside sign as 15 km. ahead, but when we had travelled a further 25 km. we guessed we had missed it. Soon after we came upon a hotel and campsite and decided to try our luck. It was not the right one but we were told we could stay there. We later found it was run by the local mafia which gave us a feeling of security, and though it meant quite a long ride by train into the city centre, this too became part of our St. Petersburg experience.

Most of my memories of earlier visits to St Petersburg had been connected with the Hermitage museum, one of the world's most memorable art galleries if you have a penchant, as I do, for the Impressionists. It took us a while to get our bearings and we didn't have nearly long enough there, but this was the first visit on which I had really had time to footslog through the city.

It was early on in the process of this when we had a less pleasant insight into this city's lifestyle. Not far from Nevsky Prospect two young men approached us. One was displaying a rather unkempt tee-shirt, clearly with the intention of selling it to me, and George was about to send him packing when he became aware that the other young man, under cover of the tee-shirt was attempting to get into my handbag. We both shouted at them and one or two passers-by looked round but did not show signs of interfering. For a moment I thought one of the men was going to attack George, but he must have thought better of it and both disappeared rather quickly. Thus we learned that you carry the minimum amount with you when walking through the city and make it look as worthless as possible. On another occasion we came across a line of youngish women selling toddlers' clothing, clearly in order to get money to buy larger sizes for their growing children.

We had intended to take a conducted tour but when we enquired at one of Intourist's hotels, we were told there weren't any. We made use of their five-star loos instead and found a one-hour tour being organised just across the road for the equivalent of £1. George preferred to potter about taking photographs and probably made the right choice as I went on the tour which had a non-stop but incomprehensible commentary.

It was time to head for Finland. I must confess I was looking forward to some of the facilities that we take for granted in the West and had been rather lacking in recent weeks. The road went through forests and more forests. Sometimes there were mushroom- or bilberry-pickers selling their wares, but surprisingly they only wanted roubles and we hadn't any left. Eventually we came to the frontier where Russian officers seemed keen to open every cupboard and drawer in the campervan. At last we crossed into no-man's-land, more forest though with a wide strip where the trees had been removed and replaced by sand on which patterns had been drawn, presumably so that it was easy to see if anyone might have crossed and disturbed them. And so into Finland.

At the frontier, a young officer took our passports, looked at us and smiled a slow Finnish smile. Then he asked dryly, "Did you have a nice time?"

The first comments in my notebook after crossing into Finland are: *great sense of liberation; everything so neat and clean.* After an overnight campsite along the way, we found we had been booked into one of Helsinki's best hotels: once again this journey was proving to be a manifestation of mega-contrasts. Not least there was the luxury of having long established friends planning for us.

----oOo----

In 1993 another chapter of my life came to an end. My friend Philippa died. Although we were of different generations, we had always got on well and I had learned a great deal from her, especially about the Jewish faith and the Holocaust.

In advancing old age she had moved to a flat in Bicester to be nearer to me, and latterly she had been acting strangely. She had once been a great theatre goer and now imagined she was holding post-theatre parties. And, though by no means a royalist, she began imagining that Prince Charles' car was parked outside her flat, and asked me to put a note under his windscreen wipers. She asked the same thing of another of her regular visitors, the pleasant lady who came to give her physiotherapy three times a week. In the end she was taken to the local hospital with an acute attack of bronchitis, and from there transferred to the psychiatric department in Oxford. Soon after she was transferred to a general ward, fell, broke her hip and clearly lost her will to live. I was listening to a concert on television playing one of her favourite pieces of music when the hospital rang to say she had died. It was just before her 90th birthday.

I arranged the funeral with the help of the Humanist Society, knowing that she did not want a religious service. I chose music that she liked and read some Edward Lear nonsense verse that appealed to her. The Humanist gentleman read the tribute which he had written with my help. There were only a few of us, but a Roman Catholic friend who came from London said it was the most spiritual funeral service she had attended, and I could not have asked for more.

Closing the century

I took over the editing of the *Deddington News* in the spring of 1994, a little delayed by the fact that in January and February of that year I paid my first visit to Australia. It was wonderful to see Sinette and Len in their fine apartment in South Perth, but it was the middle of their summer and the constant blue skies and high temperatures didn't suit me. Nevertheless, it was great to experience a new continent and the 'get-up-and-go' spirit that characterised it. It was on this occasion that Sinette told me that a long time earlier Nick had declared himself to be gay and had been in a long term partnership with a young man in New South Wales who was a few years younger and worked as an ophthalmologist in Brisbane. This had been relatively early in the days when young people 'outed' themselves with different sexual orientations and probably took his parents by surprise. I'd had gay colleagues and friends and often found them rather more congenial than straight guys.

Quite apart from the generation gap, with our lives running in such different directions, I'd lost touch with Nick over the years and it was high time I did something about it. In any case, when I eventually did meet Greg, it was clear that he had a salutary effect on Nick's somewhat volatile temperament. This was eighteen months later, while George was on a trip to Nepal with the YRC at a time when it was our autumn so I decided to pay a visit to Australia's spring, a much better choice of season. On that occasion I also visited an English friend living in Adelaide, and stayed with Nick and his partner Greg in their property near the New South Wales/Queensland border. It was in wild country and I remember checking with Nick that he had removed any of Australia's spectacular spiders that might be around.

"Never mind about spiders," Greg said. "How do you feel about snakes?"

Apparently there was a carpet snake snoozing in the ceiling above the shower, but it wasn't poisonous, stayed snoozing and was not nearly as worrying as Australia's saucer-sized spiders which moved around at the speed of lightning.

Greg and I got on well, and I wasn't bothered what they were as long as they were happy. They had taken over a rather neglected property and gradually turned it into something rather splendid. It was interesting how Nick seemed to have inherited from the Swiss side of the family that affinity with growing things, and especially trees. While Greg worked in Brisbane during the week, Nick tended their rather unkempt property and transformed it into a most attractive piece of estate. We did a lot of touring of the area, including along the Queensland's Sunshine Coast, which was a hotter and more built up version of its Spanish namesake; and nearby mountains including Mount Warning which could be seen from well out to sea. All the same, I remained convinced I was too old as well as too much of a European to adapt to this bright and relatively new country.

While I was enjoying so many new Antipodean experiences, George was having a very different time in Nepal. Some of it was perhaps a hint of things to come, taking the form of very bad back ache which, unusually, made it difficult for him to keep up with the rest of the party - not so much on the ascent as on the descent.

When this did not improve, he decided to go back to Kathmandu to see if he could get some treatment, and to this end he set off with a Sherpa and two porters. The only English the Sherpa spoke was the word 'left' so, in order to avoid confusion, George quickly taught him the word for 'right'. The Sherpas were apparently assiduous in looking after him - after all he was by now well into his seventies, and one of them insisted on holding his arm until he was quite sure it was really no longer necessary. At last in Kathmandu, and with difficulty, they found a Tibetan hotel that had been recommended and, a day or two later, George went to a massage parlour which his notes, with amusing emphasis, insisted was in no way kinky. Here, mother and daughter, one on each side of him, worked on him from his nose to the tips of his toes. Sadly, on his return bus journey to rejoin his group, his wallet was stolen and, as it contained his trekking permit, he was obliged to go back to Kathmandu. It was soon after that I received a call from him in Australia, and a few days later that we were reunited in north Oxfordshire.

It was on my return to the U.K. from this trip in November 1995 that I found a message from the Woodland Trust, a charity to which I had belonged for some years. A few acres of land, they informed me, had become available within our parish. If we could raise £9000 towards its purchase, the sum would be matched by the Millennium Fund and we would have a brand new woodland for the

Millennium. The aim was to create 200 new woods in a project called "Woods on Your Doorstep" for the millennium and this would be the first. With a forester grandfather and silviculture in my genes, how could I ignore this appeal? But it was already November, they needed the money by the end of January, the *Deddington News* did not come out in January, and the Parish Council proved to be against the project (too far, too time-taking, etc., etc.).

The Woodland Trust extended the deadline to the end of February 1996, the Parish Clerk agreed to become the recipient of any pledges of donations we could drum up, and the DN distribution team consented to deliver an appeal to every house in the parish for contributions towards the £9000. Slowly the pledges came in and the total rose from the hundreds of £s to three, five, seven thousand. Then the World Wild Life Fund gave us £500 and as we approached the £9000 mark, the Parish Council finally underwrote the last few hundreds. We'd done it!

Subsequently there were meetings at which to decide the kind of wood to be planted (all trees had to be native and, with guidance from the Woodland Trust, we settled on a riverine wood); its name - I lobbied and won with Daeda's Wood (Daeda being the Anglo Saxon tribal chief who was the first to settle on the site of Deddington), - and the year's timetable. The field currently had a barley crop so we needed to wait until it had been harvested before progressing the wood. In the end we settled on a November date in 1996 for the birth of Daeda's Wood. We awoke that day to grey skies and drizzle that turned to steady rain which stopped and, by the time we were on the site, had turned to steady snow.

The Woodland Trust had set up a marquee and a loo, and marked out scores of rows of trees and placed the saplings to be planted. The snow settled into a quietly persistent fall and from all directions families came, on foot, with their children and dogs and spades, and began to dig for Daeda. If we had needed justification, this day of enthusiastic family participation fully provided it.

A few months later, the Cherwell District Council arranged a path for wheelchair- and pram-users, and we planted a wildflower meadow. By Daeda's first birthday we learned that 90% of the original saplings had survived and thrived. The following year it found its way on to the map as we established the Deddington Circular Path passing through the wood. By 2000, Daeda's Wood was a proper wood of modest-sized trees, complete with path for wheelchair users, an otter holt to encourage the otters whose signs had been seen in the valley, and not least an active support group, The Friends of Daeda's Wood, to monitor its welfare and record its flora and fauna. In the summer of 2000 we celebrated with a well attended family picnic for the village, complete with tug-of-war and treasure hunt. It was a lovely day not marred by any sound of portable radio and without a scrap of litter left after everyone had gone home.

It was pleasing to think that I had left a mark, albeit modest, on the world map for, indeed, Daeda's Wood shortly made its appearance on the Ordnance Survey Map. I hoped my grandfather was looking upon me benevolently and forgiving me for any childhood misdeeds. We went down to look at it regularly, and of course there was no change until we crept into spring and the mini-trees began to show signs of leaf. I swore I watched a small flock of blue tits fluttering through and heard them say "hey, here's a new wood!" Well, that was my story and I was sticking to it.

----oOo----

In 1996, Prince Charles and Diana Princess of Wales divorced. Over the years, Diana's work with charities had increased and widened, notably to include the homeless, the addicted and her particular involvement with removal of the debris left behind by war, notably landmines.

In 1997 we returned to East Europe for a marathon tour approaching 7000 miles. Although we had visited all of it before, it was interesting how new things made a particular impression and how changes in circumstances had affected different countries. Czechoslovakia, for example, had become two independent states: the Czech Republic and Slovakia. The former's capital, Prague, however, remained as full of music as ever reminding me of a quotation from Mozart who apparently said that the people of Prague were the only ones who really appreciated his music; though I suspect other citizens might challenge that. Later, as we visited friends in part of what was former Yugoslavia, now called Serbia, we responded irritably to new regulations making life and, in particular, currency exchange difficult on a section of motorway.

"People used to be helpful here," I said crossly.

The young man who was trying to explain the regulation to me looked at me sadly. "Yes, I lived in that country," he said.

After brief return visits to Bulgaria and Romania, we went back to Poland noting how its ever enterprising population had adapted to its chequered return to independence. In particular we noted an intermittent rash of western cars, mainly from Germany and the Netherlands, occasionally from the U.K., whose presence was apparent in a number of camp sites. Here they were being vigorously cleaned and polished by a small army of men and their families, far into the night, before departing in convoys for various destinations, probably in the Ukraine or Russia.

Following our Polish interlude, we re-crossed the three Baltic States, finding the border formalities a good deal smoother than on our visit four years earlier. This time we decided to leave out St. Petersburg and took the ferry over the Gulf of Bothnia to Helsinki where we were met by our good friends, Matti and Ritva. Our three days at their summer cottage, enjoying virtually twenty-four hours of midsummer daylight, made a wonderful antidote to the earlier complexities of touring through twelve countries in as many weeks. It was at the end of August after our return that the tragic road accident occurred in Paris in which Princess Diana was fatally wounded followed, by an amazing period of mourning throughout the U.K.

In 1999, our final European trip of the millennium was to France and Switzerland, partly to keep in touch with my 'Swiss half'. En route for Switzerland we did a detour to one of France's war graves, which are always beautifully maintained. It was called the Ferme de Suippes set amongst a vast acreage of arable land and, along with many others, was in the Verdun area in which over 100,000 perished in World War One. This particular one had 9000 war graves from both world wars and a visitors book listing many who had travelled across the world to find the final resting place of long-ago relatives. We mused on how war had changed the nature of victims, the latter now being innumerable civilians who were guilty of nothing more than being born in the wrong place. Little did we then realise how it was about radically to change again.

In Switzerland we visited the dwindling number of my Swiss relatives - very few indeed left from my generation. On our return through France, we were reminded of another conflict from very much earlier times. We found ourselves passing close to the village of Domrémy in the upper Meuse valley whose name sign informed us: *birthplace of Joan of Arc.* The simple farmhouse where she was born and spent her childhood is now a museum. Her mother wrote that she *"grew up amid the fields and pastures. I had her baptized and confirmed and brought her up in the fear of God. I taught her respect for the traditions of the Church as much as I was able to do given her age and simplicity of her condition. I succeeded so well that she spent much of her time in church and after having gone to confession she received the sacrament of the Eucharist every month. Because the people suffered so much, she had a great compassion for them in her heart and despite her youth she would fast and pray for them with great devotion and fervour."* For all her simplicity she certainly made her mark. In the pretty church you could see where she was baptised and where she sat in the choir.

And so we returned from a pleasant but relatively uneventful trip. But I had other plans with which to start the new millennium.

At first it seemed a brilliant idea to celebrate it by taking George on a surprise return visit to South Georgia. It would be good to see the Spenceley Glacier for myself and fitting, I thought, that in advanced years he should review one of his major achievements. I spent hours amounting to days searching for something suitable on the internet. There were quite a few cruises, mostly starting from South America, but the prices were certainly not in our income bracket. I debated with myself whether this wasn't one of those occasions when one should still the small quiet voice that said *save the pennies and the pounds will look after themselves*, and similar discouragements from distant decades. Not easy. It seemed downright irresponsible to spend way beyond our means on something so self-indulgent.

Still, I continued to fail to find anything remotely within our reach, and finally confessed to George what I was up to.

"Oh, **Dar**ling!" he exclaimed enfolding me in one of his particularly memorable hugs. "That really is the loveliest thing anyone has ever tried to do for me." Later we discussed it in earnest and George finally persuaded me that marvellous though it might be in an ideal world and in ideal conditions, the greater likelihood would be that we would spend any time in South Georgia without any visibility at all, turning my brilliant surprise into the dampest imaginable squib.

"Why don't we do a world tour?" he finally came up with.

Yes, why not?

Vague plans began to take shape. George would do a final trek in Nepal; we would stay with my sister and family in Oz; then visit one of the few surviving participants of the South Georgia expedition on Vancouver Island; pay our respects to New York. It would be a dual celebration: for me for my 70th birthday just passed, and for George for his 80th, about to come; and the millennium, of course.

151

As we got down to more detail, it clearly made sense for me to go ahead to Oz while George was doing his trek. Truth to tell, he had started getting a bit vague and I wasn't that thrilled at him doing a lone trek: except that I knew he would not be alone. He would have a Sherpa guide who would look after him as if he were his own grandfather, and you couldn't be alone for long on any of the well trodden paths of Nepal. Too well trodden in the opinion of many, including George. It still felt pretty self-indulgent but also more appropriate in reflecting both our careers and bringing us in touch with family and special friends. By now we had also added New Zealand to the list. After all my parents had met when travelling to it fairly soon after World War One, and we would tour the modern traditional way, hiring a campervan to visit both North and South Islands.

For once, Sinette and Len expressed the opinion we were doing something quite sensible. Having gone through their own adventure of changing not only homes but continents and hemispheres, our plan did not sound at all preposterous, only a bit extravagant. And, after all, although we had done a great deal of travelling together, little of it had been extravagant. As we were to be away for quite a considerable time, we were delighted when two different lots of friends agreed to make use of our house in our absence. One was a friend who lived mainly in Australia but wanted to spend some time near Oxford in order to do some research. The others were our two dear Finnish friends, Matti and Ritva who would actually be there on our return.

On the whole I don't like spending Christmas away from the familiarity of my own candlelit Christmas tree, the unplanned laziness interrupted by a drink at one of the locals, phone calls to friends and members of the family, and wonderfully unproductive hours battling with crosswords. But Christmas in Nepal certainly had its moments. One of them was the pleasure of seeing the local version of a Christmas tree, covered with blobs of cotton wool to emulate its snowy western counterpart. And it was touching the way so many locals went out of their way to approach us and wish us a 'merry Christmas' in English. And perhaps memorable above all was the view of Annapurna as we lay in bed in our hotel in Pokhara.

On Boxing Day we bade each other farewell, as I set off by bus back to Kathmandu and, in due course, Australia. At that moment, the project didn't seem quite such a good idea, but it was a sensible compromise to meet the preferences of both of us. My flight via Singapore was not particularly memorable and it was grand to find

Sinette and Len and, a few days later, be able to celebrate the New Year with them for the first time in many a year. If I'd had any concerns for George they were soon dismissed when I checked my email. Several messages with unknown female signatures affirmed that he was, as usual, making friends with, to judge by the tone, the likelihood of more *rendez-vous* to come. By the time we were celebrating Australia Day on January 26th, George had joined us, satisfied with his Himalayan trek and the sundry ladies he had met, including an Iranian living in the UK, and a Hungarian Canadian living in New York. It was grand to have time with my own family, and in retrospect especially valued as it was the last time I was to see my brother-in-law Len, who died the following September.

After we left them we briefly visited a friend near Sydney and then flew on to New Zealand where we had hired a motor caravan for four weeks in order to 'do' the North and South Islands. Our New Zealand chapter began at Auckland airport where we were met by a representative of the motor caravan-hire company along with the vehicle which would be our home for the next four weeks. Compared with the basic VW campervan we had at home, this one was very sophisticated and well equipped. The rep gave us a comprehensive introduction to it all and then directions on how to reach the camp site where we would spend our first night. For reasons I can't remember I'd offered to do this short drive. However well explained, route directions never seem as straight forward as you think, and I was also somewhat discomfited by a red light on the dashboard.

"What *d'you* think that is?" I asked George, but his guess was as good as mine.

It seemed to take ages, but we found the camp site, chose a pitch, sorted out the basics and then checked the vehicle's handbook to discover we were out of oil!

We explored Auckland a bit and then set off for Rotorua. I remembered Mum describing it as an explosive sort of place, as much of the North Island is and, indeed, it had recently sent up a massive hot water spout which was described to us by locals as simply clearing its throat. We went to see the place - about the size of a football pitch - in which the trees were turned into ghostly grey by a covering of ash, and rocks were strewn everywhere. I rather hoped this sort of display did not materialise too frequently. We also visited a Maori village and thermal area where the Pohutu geyser steamed away quietly but put on a fairly predictable and more impressive hourly eruption for several minutes. It means 'big splash' and is not ill named as it is the largest in the southern hemisphere. The neat houses of the Maori village itself were punctuated by more modest springs.

There are some very good museums in the area, both regarding Maori history and, if you have a penchant for the earth's more erratic behaviour, remarkable displays and films giving the how-and-why of volcanoes and earthquakes. At the time of our visit there was a particularly riveting display and film at the Volcanic Activity Centre at Wairaki, but much of New Zealand's North Island is a living museum to geological activity since, situated as it is on the boundary of both the Australian and Pacific tectonic plates, there is probably a great deal more of such activity than its inhabitants might wish for.

It was a three-hour crossing from New Zealand's North to South Island. The latter is less explosive than its northern counterpart but scenically more spectacular, featuring the country's highest peaks, including Mount Cook, and some very fine national parks. One of these includes two splendid glaciers, the Franz Josef and the Fox. We saw both of these though not under the best conditions. The South Island also provided George with a good excuse to get to the top of something, in this case Mount Roy which he chose as being rather easy by his standards. I dropped him off at the starting point and picked him up after a day of gentle pottering and writing.

Among other things, I wanted to revisit some of the places that must have become familiar to my mother when she travelled here so many decades earlier, in the process meeting my father. I cursed myself that I had not asked her for more detail of her activities. The most I knew was that she had spent most of her time in Dunedin on the South Island, but I did not even know the name of the family who had employed her and whose descendants might, indeed, be still living there.

One of the city's main sights is the Otago Settlers Museum, arguably one of the best in New Zealand. It covers the story of pretty well all comers to New Zealand, their life styles and effect on each other. The Maori were the first arriving in the second half of the 13th century. Next came the Europeans in the early 19th century, though mainly from the middle of that century with the arrival of the Scottish Lay Association who founded Dunedin and named it after the first syllables of Dundee and Edinburgh. There was also a substantial Chinese settlement, initially by those seeking their fortune and taking over sites abandoned by Europeans, and later, in the 1930s, by a younger generation choosing to distance themselves geographically from Communism.

The other 'must' is the Royal Albatross Centre on the Otago peninsular which has the world's only mainland breeding colony of this amazing species. The peninsula was also home to a wide variety of sea birds as well as seals and penguins, especially blue and yellow-eyed penguins. We had the pleasure of watching several of the latter making their way up a steep cliff to their nests, built there because of the protective vegetation and lower temperatures it offered. Not the most agile of creatures on land, the penguins would struggle up to a certain height then rest, gazing out at sea until they had caught enough breath to continue. In fact it was amusing here and there on the South Island to see signs reading 'Beware of Penguins', not because they were any danger to us but because we might be a danger to them.

And so, via Honolulu, to Vancouver.

----oOo----

In Vancouver we had a pleasant guide, who gave us a whistle-stop morning tour of the city then took us to lunch at a restaurant famous for its oysters. George regarded these with some misgivings as he doesn't have the best relationship with shell fish. But on this occasion, he was not the one to fall foul of them. Soon after lunch our guide gave a grunt, turned swiftly into a parking lot and promptly collapsed at the wheel. I'm not sure how but we found out there was a hospital nearby and George managed to fathom out the route to it. With some relief we unloaded our poorly guide in the equivalent of A&E, gave them all the information we could and resumed our sightseeing. We revisited the patient later in the day and learned he had food poisoning and would we please call his girl friend to tell her what had happened.

But our main reason for visiting Canada was to see Stan Paterson, a glaciologist and one of the few surviving members of George's South Georgia expedition. He and his partner Lyn lived on Quadra, an island off Vancouver Island, reached by a short flight to Campbell River. George and Stan hadn't seen each other for a long time so the air buzzed with reminiscences. We spent most of our brief visit walking, talking and bird watching, very relaxing after so much travelling. Checking email, we learned that foot-and-mouth which had begun before we left the UK had spread, and Daeda's Wood was now closed. It put things in perspective when we returned to Vancouver and found that an earthquake in Seattle had been felt there. That evening the television gave dire warnings of the worst winter storms in New York for decades .... Somehow we weren't surprised! We seemed to attract weird weather.

From Vancouver our journey to New York involved a change of planes at Montreal, and it was here that we had our next minor hiccup: New York's main airport was closed due to heavy snowfalls. It also appeared that immigration for the United States would take place at Montreal airport. The airline kindly put us up at a very nice hotel and informed our hotel in New York that we would be late; in fact it became 'two days late', shrinking our five-night stay to three!

A very helpful woman at the transport desk at New York's La Guarda airport told us the best way to travel into the city was to book on to a shuttle cab - one that would take several people thus considerable reducing the cost. We had a cheery black driver and three other passengers including a couple from Iowa (*'we guess you guys won't know where that is?' - 'Oh yes, we do - we canoed through it!' 'You're* **kidding!'***)*. The other passengers were dropped first, and I have to say that the taxi driver looked rather nonplussed as he drew up at the door of the address we had given him. It's true that it did not look very inviting; however, the driver rang the bell, was assured that we were expected, and helped us to unload our luggage.

We were taken up to the next floor and shown our room: a smallish room pretty well entirely filled by a Queen size double bed. OK, so it wasn't luxury, but nor was it a luxury price, and it was clean. We had no complaints. So we did what we usually did: a minimum of unpacking then went to explore our surroundings. We were rather surprised to come upon a long line which proved to be a food queue which we were told a woman ran as a charity on Sundays and Wednesdays for the poor. Indeed, the area seemed to be a mixture of extremely humble flats and expensive-looking apartment blocks, the latter patently not providing easy access to the casual visitor. We had chosen the location because it was described as East Village but subsequently an American friend told us that more accurately it was referred to as Alphabet City, so-called because most of the street names included a letter of the alphabet.

The next three days were very full. We spent the first morning establishing a route (by bus and subway) into Manhattan and an all-too-short visit to the Grand Metropolitan Art Museum (which, like the Hermitage in St. Petersburg, really needed a minimum a couple of days). We then met one of the girl friends George had acquired in

Nepal a few years earlier, who took us to Grand Central Station, a sightseeing highlight in its own right.

On the second day I headed for a lunchtime Fellowship meeting, arranging to meet up with George in the afternoon. The meeting was huge - probably nearly a hundred. Early on they asked visitors to introduce themselves, so I announced myself as Sylvie from Banbury in England, at which a woman a little younger than me a couple of rows in front turned and told me not to leave after the meeting until we had spoken. She proved to be Lorna and English though she had lived in the U.S. much of her life. We had a lunch snack together and forged the beginning of a friendship that was to last until her stroke fifteen years later. I caught up with George in Times Square and we spent the rest of our brief time in New York seeing as much as we could, one of the best trips being a harbour cruise for a spectacular view of the Manhattan's sky-scraping skyline (including the ill-fated Twin Towers), the Statue of Liberty and passing under Brooklyn Bridge. My notes referred to it as 'a must' for anyone on a short visit.

And so farewell to North America and, indeed, the rest of the world. It was wonderful quite a few hours later to be greeted at Banbury bus station by Matti and Ritva and return to an impeccably kept house and a splendid meal that made us welcome guests in our own home.

But the first year of the new millennium had not quite finished with us. In December the name of Daeda's Wood echoed round the Halls of Westminster. The occasion was a reception in the House of Commons, hosted by Paddy Tipping, M.P. for that other little wood Sherwood Forest. It was to celebrate the achievement of the Woodland Trust of 200 new woods for the Millennium. As the first of the Woods on Your Doorstep, Daeda's Wood received several honourable mentions as did the Friends of Daeda's Wood as a shining example of community commitment. I preened on behalf of us all.

9/11 and beyond

On returning from our world tour, there wasn't much opportunity to pause and catch our breaths. The amount of correspondence, now considerably swollen by email, was prodigious. The YRC had elected to accept George's suggestion and chose Yugoslavia as the venue for their overseas climbing meet, and he needed to circulate information. In fact, it was no longer Yugoslavia but 'former Yugoslavia', split into the several republics which had formerly composed it: Slovenia, Croatia, Serbia with Montenegro, Bosnia-Herzegovina, Macedonia. The YRC had settled for Slovenia as having the best mountains, indeed the highest in former Yugoslavia. The meet was scheduled for September. About a dozen had booked in for it and we had agreed to use the camp site at Bohinjska Bistrica, an old favourite of ours. Most people were travelling by car, and I had decided to travel to Slovenia, too, stay with the group for a few days and then go on to meet my Bosnian friend Sveto and his wife in Serbia before travelling on to Sarajevo.

Sveto had finally left Sarajevo after threats to his life and settled in Novi Sad. I felt for him. We were about the same age, and to be obliged to leave the place which had been your lifetime home and, at approaching seventy, start again elsewhere in a divided country was tough. Not that he would have a problem starting again elsewhere. He was a respected academic, formerly head of a university department, wrote and translated books.

I was going to stay with him and his wife in Novi Sad, and he met me off the bus at Belgrade and drove me to their high-rise block where they had managed to re-create their Bosnian home. They had plenty of tales too of the bombing of Serbia by the U.N. during the civil war, and I felt for this small country which always seemed to be on 'the wrong side'. One story was of a young man who had been out drinking late with his friends and suddenly remembered he should be home with his extremely expectant wife. He had hurried to cross one of the bridges over the Danube, after being warned against it as all the bridges were potential bombing targets. He had been half way across when the bomb hit making his child fatherless even before it was born.

Sveto had warned me he couldn't face driving right into Sarajevo, but he would drive me to the outskirts whence I could catch a bus. In the event, he drove me into the centre, and indicated the building housing the bed-and-breakfast place into which I'd booked. My landlady spoke no English but some French and, with my smattering of Serbo Croat, we managed.

Snežka, one of Sveto's university teaching friends got in touch with me and came to pick me up at nine o'clock next morning. We wandered round the bazaar area, much more commercialised than I remembered it; drank a lot of coffee and talked and talked. She was fascinating to talk to as she had spent a lot of the siege in Sarajevo, for much of which her husband was in hiding as he did not want to be conscripted into the Bosnian army. They had stayed partly because the in-laws were too old and frail to move, and partly while they waited to find a way to get their children to safety in the U.K. I asked her what she thought of the Serbs' part in the horrors of which we heard, and she responded by asking whether we had also heard of the hundreds of thousands of Serbs who had been expelled from Croatia. And worse.

"Once the country began to split ethnically, it was not possible to think of anything but how best to preserve your own family and culture. In many cases where there were mixed marriages, if there were no children the couples split and each went back to their ethnic group. Mostly the middle-aged and old have stayed." After a moment she added sadly "It is a mess."

While we sat in the open air cafe in the bazaar, Snežka pointed out a lot of young men with that dark part-shaven look associated with the Middle East and as we had become used to seeing on films of the Taliban. "Many are Afghans. They were here too during the fighting." Later we learned how much the war had been supported by certain Moslem countries in the Middle East.

On my second afternoon, I was sitting writing postcards in my room when Madame came in looking agitated. "*Venez, venez ... tout de suite...* " she said, beckoning violently for added emphasis. Puzzled, I followed her into the living room where she stood pointing at the television set.

Why on earth was she showing me pictures of aeroplanes flying into skyscrapers, I wondered. *And the same pictures, over and over again?*

And then the screen informed me that I was watching CNN and a Canadian voice told me in appalled tones that I was witnessing the events of 9/11 as they were unfolding in New York.

I slumped into a chair while Madame chattered beside me, mainly in Serbo-Croat now. After a while I went to the window and looked out on to the streets of this city that had experienced so much death and heartache, and marvelled at the normality of the scene. On the television screen the airliner kept plunging into the same building, and down on the streets of New York, crowds ran for their lives pursued by clouds of dust and debris. Then another airliner crashed into a second tower block. Suddenly I wished I could talk to George and wondered if the YRC group in Slovenia were aware of these world-shaping events.

I stayed watching the television for much of the rest of the day. It was very repetitive and with a depressing preoccupation with the state of the international money markets, but in between we saw, over and over again, one after the other the Twin Towers collapse and the mayhem of dust and panic on the streets of New York as its shattered inhabitants struggled to come to terms with what was happening.

The following morning I took a tram to Ilidža a few kilometres away, scene of the assassination of the Archduke Franz Ferdinand which had triggered World War One. It seemed as though the whole of 20th century history was being telescoped into this small Balkan setting, only a few months into the 21st. A lot of the hotels were boarded up, and there were many signs warning of mines, so I decided it was probably not the best time for exploration. On the way back into the city I stopped at the Holiday Inn. We could have been anywhere in the world, though judging from the dress of the clientele crowding the foyer we might as well have been in any one of a number of Middle Eastern cities. No one seemed to be paying much attention to the repeating images of the collapsing Twin Towers on the television screen.

Later Snežka took me to her flat which was on the tenth floor of an 18-floor building. The front of it looked over the main street and had a massive hole where one of the windows should be. Beyond the main street rose the mountains from which the Serb army had fired on to the city. Snežka explained that a lot of the flats had been used by Bosnian snipers to fire at the Serbs; - by Bosnian she meant Bosniak as the Bosnians of the Islamic faith were known.

The family had moved to the rest of the flat, away from the main street. She described how, one after the other, the shops had closed as there was nothing to sell. Rations distributed by the U.N. were largely nicked and sold on the black market. The other problem was firewood. Supplies of electricity had ceased early on so this was needed for cooking. Once the trees had been cut down in the city, the bold went up on to the mountains at night. Snežka said she had become very adept at identifying which were the best bundles of firewood on offer. And then there was the water which needed collecting from standpipes, every journey risking life and limb at any road junction that was exposed to the fighters entrenched in the hills.

But one of the most difficult problems of all occurred when a flat became empty for then it was immediately taken over by refugees and later became the subject of ongoing conflict as the original owners tried to retrieve their home. I listened to all this, wondering how people kept their sanity with so many demands made on them every day. And then I thought of Mum who, every day for months, years, of World War Two, had seen us off to school and Dad off to work, not being entirely sure that she would see us again.

That evening my hostess' boyfriend escorted me to the bus station where I boarded the bus for Ljubljana, travelling via Travnik and Banja Luka. The bus driver let me stretch out on the back seat and I slept fitfully. But there was a great sense of relief as we drove into Ljubljana. George had been held up by a road accident, but I was never more profoundly grateful to feel the security of that familiar hug than when we eventually found each other.

----oOo----

The terrorist attack on 9/11 had almost unimaginable repercussions as much of the world - and in particular the U.S. and U.K. - edged towards war under the auspices of retribution. Iraq, under the dictatorship of Saddam Hussein, was considered to be responsible for the attack; indeed Hussein was known as a brute responsible for the death of countless of his own people. Teams were dispatched to Iraq to trace the weapons of mass destruction he was deemed to possess, threatening invasion if they were not renounced. None was found and people in their millions marched in protest against such an attack which, nevertheless, took place in March, 2003. The campaign was described as Shock and Awe, and no one who saw the newsreels of that night could argue with the description.

Most people rejoiced at the removal of Saddam Hussein, but alas insufficient planning or even thought seems to have gone into 'so what next?'. An appalling tyrant he certainly was but under his rule of fear comparative order existed and the dreadful actions that eventually followed between the different factions of Islam were contained. As

161

these factions grew in power, often with assistance from other powers with axes to grind, so did the break-away groups that resulted with ever-growing arsenals of weapons and, more terrible still, the will to sacrifice themselves for their cause. In time the focus of the different factions extended from inflicting harm on each other to taking revenge on those who had triggered the profound deprivation and unrest that characterised much of the Middle East, a process made easier by the advances in technology which enabled hatred and planning to be spread by the click of a button.

No doubt there were many actions of which we never heard, but one of the first to impact on the western world was the attack on Madrid's railways whose human toll was 181 dead and over 1800 injured in March, 2004. The following year it was London's turn.

In the meantime, towards the end of the 2002 in Deddington, I was having coffee with Marianne when she said, "Judy has a sabbatical next year and wants to do a house swap so she and Alan can come over here for three months. I could put a note in the D.N. to ask if anyone might be interested - what do you think?" Judy was her daughter and she and her partner Alan worked for the local university and lived in Ogden in the state of Utah. This was where the Mormons had finally settled after being hounded out of several other places. Indeed we had visited one of them - in Nauvoo - when canoeing the Mississippi and stayed with a charming Mormon family.

"Let me think about it," I said.

George had started getting lunch when I got home. I asked, "How would you feel about spending three months in Utah next year?"

I well knew what the answer would be. We started negotiations straight away, settling on the period May-July which meant that George would not miss his lecture season. We were to swap cars as well as houses, so appropriate insurance needed to be arranged. Judy and Alan planned to stay for a couple of days after our arrival, which meant they could familiarise us with all we needed to know, including their two cats: Betsy who was a true softie and Willow who was an extremely aloof Siamese. We knew it would be very hot for much of our stay, but happily their home had a cooler subterranean level which could also be turned into another bedroom.

And so, on 20th May 2003, we landed in Salt Lake City, were met at the airport by Judy and Alan, and driven to our new temporary home. It was a pleasant well-equipped bungalow in a leafy neighbourhood, with loads of space. Naturally it was a huge advantage having Judy and Alan there for a couple of days during which they showed us how everything worked and made sure we could drive their automatic, four-wheel drive Subaru. Judy had also sorted out for me a list of local Fellowship meetings and introduced me to a member who was a great friend.

All the same it seemed quite odd when the taxi came to collect them for the airport and we turned back to the empty house that was now 'ours'. Gradually we settled into a routine. I approached the local paper to ask if they would like an occasional article on a foreigner's eye view of their community and they said they would. My first article included our interest in local bird life after which we were immediately contacted by the Audubon Society (a sort of US equivalent of the RSPB) who said they met regularly for an early breakfast and bird watching trip - would we like to join? And of course we did which was a pleasant way of getting to know a group of like-minded people as well as familiarising ourselves with our surroundings. On our return from such ventures, Betsy would trot towards us purring loudly. She had a prodigious purr with which she would approach us each in turn so that we would each think we were the favoured one until we realised it was a ploy for getting the greatest fuss made of her. Willow was far too superior for this and relied (successfully) on us regarding her most casual attention as a special favour. I also took Judy's place in a book-reading group which meant I read a vast modern novel which I would not otherwise have read and by an author whom I did not know. I did not particularly enjoy the books, but it got me to meet another pleasant group of people.

George chose to rise at an extremely early hour to go for a run. We would have breakfast on his return, by which time the heat of the day was already apparent and, unless we had plans, we did not do a great deal. If we did go for an excursion it was likely to be into the Wasatch mountains where it was cooler.

We also quite soon went to Salt Lake City, Utah's capital and dominated by its Temple. The Mormons trace their origins to the 1820s when Joseph Smith was led by visions to seek the teachings of the Book of Mormon inscribed on golden plates. In 1838 they turned swampland on the shores of the Mississippi into the Mormon centre of Nauvoo and here built a great temple. After the murder of Joseph Smith, his followers set off across the frozen Mississippi to find a place where they could pursue their faith in peace. It was some years, including journeys of great hardship by wagon across inhospitable land, before they came to the site of Salt Lake City led by Brigham Young where he is recorded as stating, "This is the right place."

The approach to it along which thousands of settlers built their homes became known as the Mormon Corridor. In what was to become Salt Lake City, the site of the Mormon Tabernacle was rapidly established and today is part of the soaring structures of the Mormon Temple. The tabernacle choir was created even before the building was complete and is renowned for its concerts. It could be heard rehearsing every Sunday. The museums of the Temple area showed the incredible hardships endured by the early settlers - not only those travelling by covered wagon from the east, but those subsequently arriving from Europe and surviving - one wonders how - the horrendous conditions on board ships in which babies were born and many travellers died. But, of course, as far as many of them were concerned, they were travelling to Zion 'the promised land', home of a lost tribe of Israel.

We decided to take a look at just how inhospitable the approaches to Salt Lake City were from the east, and followed the dead-straight road across the Salt Lake desert. There are a few lumps and bumps in the landscape, but otherwise it is flat, flat, flat, the brush dying out until you just have the bright white sand and the twin ribbons of the Interstate 80 (Chicago to San Francisco), shadowed by the railway. It is a huge and largely empty area and part of it provides the setting for the Bonneville Speedway established here in 1914 and where many a speed record has been broken. Here, too, is Wendover Airfield which, during World War Two, was the training site of the 509th Composite Group, the B-29 unit that carried out the atomic bombings of Hiroshima and Nagasaki. A commemorative plaque quotes President Truman's comment *The atomic bomb is too dangerous to be loose on a lawless world. We thank God that it has come to us.* An interesting perspective from the era itself.

Another unexpected aspect was that, despite gambling being against the law in Utah, Wendover straddled the border with Nevada's border and was a hive of casinos. We went to take a look at them on another day and patronised one of the gaming establishments where we found ourselves in a huge hall, dimly lit but with sparkling lights winking over batteries of fruit machines. A woman, who was obviously a *habitué,* showed me the ropes and in no time I had the brief pleasure of gambling (and losing) my self-imposed quota of $6.

She was clearly astounded and dismayed when I walked away, deciding that was enough.

There were also unusual historic sites down in the plateau scrubland to the east of the Wasatch mountains. One is the Golden Spike Memorial Park, marking the point where, remarkably, the First Transcontinental Railroad's two sections finally came together on 10th May, 1869, for the-first time linking the continent's East and West, though not yet the Atlantic and Pacific oceans. Work on this had begun in 1866 as the Union Pacific and Central Pacific began forging a route from Omaha to Sacramento. Not surprisingly the two lines ended up way past each other. Over 11,000 Chinese labourers were employed among the many thousands more of immigrant labour, including especially Irish, German and Italian. Harsh winters, intense summer heat, Indian raids and the rough and tumble of frontier life made for wretched conditions and there were many deaths. But finally, the Federal Government stepped in to insist on a negotiated meeting point and the two lines met at Promontory Summit to form one continuous track.

Over the following century, the rail route was changed - the old rails of this section were even salvaged for the war effort in 1942. After World War II, local residents began marking the remarkable achievement with a re-enactment of the driving of the last spike completing the linking of the original railroads, and the area has been turned into a memorial park where the Golden Spike ceremony is re-enacted regularly in the tourist season and on special occasions.

In addition to its Mormon history, Utah is also known for its red rock country and a scattering of very fine State Parks protecting it. We had thought it would be pleasant to spend a week touring some of these and, before leaving the U.K., I had approached some motor home magazines asking if they would be interested in an article on such a tour. One of them was, so we set a date for this adventure. Compared with our modest VW campervan at home, our loaned vehicle was like a palace, which made for a very comfortable adventure indeed.

The State Parks were spectacular. The rock was indeed mainly red, but there were other colours going all the way from rose to cinnamon, lemon to flame, ash to purple. We visited five parks and we both voted Bryce State Park as the best, for colour and drama. A path runs along the rim of the immeasurable acres of its canyons weathered by millennia into curves and whorls as of man-made sculptures. Temples, almost. Only no human hand had ever wielded a chisel in that unforgiving place.

.   "I wonder what Ebenezer Bryce thought of it," I mused aloud "You're making him up."

"You obviously haven't read the brochure. Ebenezer Bryce and his family moved here in 1875 and made the road up to this plateau to harvest the timber. So they named the canyon after him. Apparently he said it would be a hell of a place to lose a cow."

"It would be a hell of a place to lose anything."

On another occasion we visited Yellowstone Park, the world's first national park, covering over 2.2 million acres. Initially it was a little disappointing. As I've said, I like trees, but the endless and uncountable acres of coniferous forests became initially tedious, then boring, then downright oppressive. And when there was a view it was of more and more and yet more of dark green stretching into infinity ... until suddenly the dark green was replaced by unutterably drab grey.

"That'll be those fires," said George who mostly does read about places before he goes to them. "In 1988. Dozens of little ones that became several big ones and they went on all summer."

We learned some of the fires were started by humans but by far the greater number were the result of lightning strikes. At the peak of the disaster, over 9,000 fire fighters were involved from as far afield as Alaska and Hawaii, and the last flames only extinguished when the weather changed in September and it *snowed.*

Yes, from our trip down the Mississippi we knew about America's extreme weather, but this was something else, especially when allied to Yellowstone's volcanic nature for this is one of the most restless places on the planet. There are three calderas created dating back up to a million or two years ago; the eruptions which created them sent huge quantities of ash covering most of central America. It's said that the next time it blows there will be enough ash to block out the sun, disrupting the global climate enough to create food shortages and mass famine. I found myself hoping that the next eruption wouldn't come too soon.

Our time in Utah was approaching its end. We found that we had really begun to feel integrated in that corner of the U.S. largely born out of persecution elsewhere and full of intense, sometimes strange beliefs contrasting with the very laid-back nature of the place. Many of the friends we had made were lapsed Mormons, often known as Jack Mormons, though they still retained some of the characteristics ingrained in the believers: integrity, helpfulness and a wry sense of humour. One we met, who in his believing days had been a missionary in Europe, told us of an incident in Germany when he had been harangued at length by a woman for the American treatment of the Blacks. He listened patiently and then quietly returned with 'And now, Madam, shall we discuss the Jews?'!

Like many other areas of the U.S., Utah is dinosaur country. There is rather a good dinosaur park in Ogden itself where realistic models move and roar so convincingly that we saw more than one small child cling to its parents in alarm. There are also other dinosaur-orientated sites and we visited one on a short tour from Ogden beginning on a fine day that took us to nearly 9,500 feet at Wolf Creek Summit, then descending eventually to join and follow the Duchesne river. The latter feeds a broadening valley made fertile by batteries of great sprinklers, rather like some mad robotic army sending its jets - some of them rotating - arching over the fields. It was a valley of well scattered small ranches mainly of cattle and horses.

And so we entered dinosaur country. Near Vernal there is a Dinosaur Monument with a section in Utah and another in a small community called Dinosaur (yes, really) in neighbouring Colorado. Some of the scenery is a bit reminiscent of a gigantic quarry. The Monument covers over 200,000 acres in which there are tens of thousands of fossils and ongoing excavations. The Visitors' Centres and museums have excellent displays illustrating the age of planet earth, when and which dinosaurs existed and for how long up to 150 million years ago, compared with the punier presence of man. For those interested in the 'why' and 'how' of the way things happen, it was fascinating to learn that a hundred years or so ago the scene would have been very different: the predominant sage and brush would have been replaced by a great grassy plains. The reason for this was the frequency of fire from which grass recovered much more quickly. It was when man came and used the grasslands for grazing that erosion set in and caused brush to predominate.

Soon it was time to start thinking of our return home, which initially meant making sure that we left our friends' home in a tidy and welcoming condition. The cats were soon aware that change was in the offing and Willow in particular became adept at placing herself precisely where it would be difficult not to tread on her. When we started opening suitcases, Betsy promptly sat in them and miouwed plaintively.

Our last few days were extremely sociable, meeting and saying farewell to our new friends, including two who had just returned from the U.K. during which they had stayed in our house. Then came the final pack watched by a pair of sulking cats.

----oOo----

It had been quite soon after our return home from our historic visit to former Yugoslavia in 2001 that the embryo of an idea for a novel began to gain momentum in my head. In my fictional themes I had always been less interested in the dysfunctional than exploring what happened to ordinary people in extraordinary circumstances. In particular I wanted to explore the effects of war on the children or grandchildren of participants. By now it was clear that the digital world was here to stay. An increasing number of people were glued to smart-phones or tablets whose activities seemed to interrupt what used to be normal social occasions. All the same, the editing of documents had clearly become infinitely less time-taking.

So, what would happen, I wondered, if a child from war-torn Sarajevo during the former Yugoslavia's civil war was fostered by a British journalist and his wife and came to live in middle England? The idea took on a life of its own. I could visualise the child, and in due course picture her wandering round an English village that bore a remarkable resemblance to Deddington. This, I decided, would be the home of a journalist who specialised in the uneasy history of the Balkans, and his wife. It would be convenient if the couple were childless.

My main problem was that one or two of the characters tended to take over and moved in directions that weren't originally intended. The child from war-torn Sarajevo was not a problem. In my mind she was twelve, called Jasminka, and had lost her father to sniper fire. Jasminka, after renaming herself Minkie, slowly adapted to her new life. It was her foster mother who began to change the goalposts by having an affair with a man from her past. Minkie herself grew into a teenager and fell for an American student. She wouldn't make a decision about her future until she has revisited Sarajevo, under the illusion that her mother had died in the civil war. During the visit, with the American, she found her mother alive. The visit also coincided with the events of 9/11, leaving both young people needing to make unexpected decisions.

The more I thought about it, the more I was taken by this idea of a book based on modern history - almost a turning back of the clock as what was now called 'former Yugoslavia' had split into its component parts. Having tried the self-publishing route with *The Big Muddy* I decided to continue on it, though first I had to turn my idea into something more than a few pages of notes. It was a book I much enjoyed writing, for my visits to former Yugoslavia extended back over forty years, I knew most parts of it quite well, and could even get by with hesitant Serbo-Croat. Not only that but I had the benefit of knowing someone who had lived through several months of the siege of Sarajevo and was prepared to share his experience with me. So, while we adapted to life in Deddington, my book grew. I called it *Another Kind of Loving*, based on the love of a mother who was prepared to send her child to live with strangers to protect her from the horrors of civil war.

All the same, I knew I had to visit once more. The trip in 2001 had been indelibly memorable for the events of 9/11, but I needed to see the rest of the country and get an idea of how it was faring now, a decade after the worst of the in-fighting. So, in 2004, we planned a visit to Turkey in our new campervan, deviating through most of the six new republics that replaced former Yugoslavia. Periodically I asked one of our guides or one of the camp workers whether things had changed much. Most of them shrugged and said, "not really...."

So what had all that been about then?

But in fact, it *had* changed. Villages were in ruins as were individual houses, and everywhere, especially near the coast, new buildings were replacing them. And of course every few hundred kilometres we had to stop to go through frontier controls that had not existed before.

George found that Turkey had changed beyond recognition too. He had loved his trips there in the 1960s and was rather appalled at the extent of the developments, especially along the south coast. Equally unattractive were the mountains of exposed and reddening European flesh that dominated most resorts. There was rather a shortage of camp sites so we treated ourselves to inexpensive bed-and-breakfasts.

We returned home with another far more pleasant memory. On one of his trips forty years earlier, George and friends had ventured into a more remote area of the Taurus mountains, now forming the chief attraction of a National Park. We deviated to stop at what we considered to be the Park's centre.

169

A young man approached us to ask if we spoke English. "I am a mountain guide," he said. "Can I help?"

Indeed he could. George produced a photograph he had taken all those years ago and, amazed, the young man exclaimed, "But that is my grandfather, Ibrahim Safak. I am his grandson, Basar.

Ibrahim Safak had been the muleteer for George's party as well as their host in what had then been a primitive home. Much excitement followed our meeting with Basar and we were guided to the well-built stone house to meet his father Ali, the young donkey boy who so long ago had guided George and his friends to a high bivouac site through the Nerpiz Gorge into the cirque at Yalacik. Then a young boy of little education, now speaking good English, he was a retired schoolmaster running, with his son Basar, a small pension for trekkers.

It was a highly emotional reunion; tears of joy ran down Ali's face, there were kisses and embraces. "I am so happy," he kept repeating. It felt like the return of a much-loved, long lost relative, and his memory was remarkable. "Your car was blue," he said, "and you sent my father an electric torch,"

And so we were welcomed as of old, well fed but now in comfort at a table, and there were showers, beds and, of course, as before, to offer payment would have been offensive. Such laws of hospitality in the East still survived.

Still learning

We were to have another decade together.

On our return to Deddington from the United States, George got down to serious work planning his lecture season and I now returned to the draft of my first novel and a more serious appraisal of where I was going with it. As I had decided to stay on the self-publishing route I made contact with Tanya at Antony Rowe Ltd. for quotations and an approximate timetable. The latter really took me by surprise for such were advances in technology that apparently I could expect a proof copy of it within about a month of sending them a pdf file of the text and organising the appropriate art work for the cover. It began to feel very exciting. In the meantime, I explored what the Internet had to offer in the way of promotion as well as the potential offered by local markets, literary festivals and reading groups.

So finally the day came when I held that proof copy of my first novel in my hands in our kitchen in Deddington and it was one of the more special moments of my life. The most time-taking and least attractive part of the whole process was promoting the book, though in time, and more pleasantly, promotion brought me in contact with fellow writers with whom it was enjoyable to compare notes.

One in particular, who remained a good friend until his too-early recent death, shared a table with me at a local literary festival. Ian Mathie specialised in Africa in various parts of which he had lived both as a child and as an adult as a professional water engineer so that he knew the continent 'from the inside' and very enlightening his books are as a result. Local markets have proved good venues, especially initially, as I knew a lot of people and they were probably a bit curious. This was helped by reasonable coverage in the local papers especially if it included a photograph. And, in due course, entering the talks market, of which more later, provided an additional means of promotion. Indeed I eventually sold all 1500 copies of *The Big Muddy* and reprinted it in 2006, when I added a collection of photographs to illustrate our journey.

Another happening around this time arose from George's Millennium trek in Nepal. He had made a considerable number of contacts, especially ladies, among fellow trekkers amazed by his age, but he had also met a man from the Netherlands who in due course visited the U.K. and came to have tea with us in Deddington. He introduced us to a splendid organisation called Servas created after World War Two with the imposing aim of discouraging further wars. This was to be done by like-minded people getting together so that no one would want to fight anyone any more, a noble if not totally realistic ambition.

Servas' like-minded members could contact each other and eventually meet in each other's homes. The stay would be free but limited to two nights unless those concerned mutually wanted to make it longer. In order to join, you needed to pay a modest annual fee and fill in a form giving your full details. This would be vetted and you would be interviewed by an established member - this to discourage those who were simply looking for a free holiday. Your membership fee entitled you to a copy of the Servas membership list in the country you wanted to visit.

We decided to become members, but before we had an opportunity to make use of it, George decided to make yet another trip to Nepal - after all, what else would you think of doing as you approached your mid-eighties! This time he elected to take himself round the Annapurna circuit, and I elected to spend the same period visiting the family in Australia, my first since Len's death. It was good to see Sinette's new home and learn about the Claire's and Mike's new project.

Together with a small group of like-minded volunteers they had become deeply involved in a charity which they ended up running called Animal Companions. This provided trained Therapy dogs to visit people in hospitals, aged care and special needs facilities, schools, prisons and psychiatric units, as well as special visits on request, for mental health and wellness events for university students and other groups.. Between 2002 and 2018, the number of volunteers has grown from nine to 140. Then, in 2007, Claire and Mike became involved in Guide Dogs WA raising three puppies to become working Guide Dogs; they still provide temporary boarding when necessary.

.   Following our application to join Servas, we were interviewed by a solicitor in Oxford, in due course accepted and, in 2007, decided this could provide a great way of exploring the American West. We planned to fly to L.A., hire a car, drive south to the Mexican border, then to the east side of the Rockies, north to the Canadian border, west to the Californian coast and south back to L.A., a total of about 6000-7000 miles of driving! By then we had also got the Servas membership book for the U.S.A. and decided to alternate stays with members with stays in cheap motels. It worked a treat.

The fact that members listed their interests was an enormous help. Not surprisingly all of them were interested in travel, many in the environment and anything to do with it, quite a few in some kind of spiritual belief, reading, walking, and so on. We decided to approach Servas members who might be on the first ten days of our route, and emailed them: the first in Chula Vista near the Mexican border, and the second in Ivins, in the southernmost corner of Utah.

But first we had to get there. We had heard that immigration control at L.A. could be quite tricky and we found ourselves at the back of a long queue to go through immigration. A uniformed lady directed us through another exit normally reserved for U.S. residents where an avuncular officer took a record of my finger prints and eyes.

Then he looked over at George and came out with the astonishing statement "I guess y'all are too old to have finger prints!" and let us through, 'y'all' in this case meaning George. We went on puzzling over our ageing fingers for a long time.

We had booked in at a nearby motel. Fortunately we were on the south side of L.A. which would not involve us driving through the city. And so, after a relatively uneventful journey, we arrived at the home of our first hosts in Chula Vista. They were charming and proved typical of all our Servas hosts who, however simple or elaborate their home, were unfailingly warm in their welcome - and we stayed in a total of just over twenty. We had made a decision in advance of our visits that we would take our hosts out to a meal while we were with them and this was always appreciated. There was also an understanding that hosts did not have to 'entertain' their guests but got on with their lives, so we often joined them at some meeting or on an expedition if appropriate.

As planned, we alternated our Servas stays with nights in cheap motels which gave us an opportunity to re-organise our luggage and get our notes up to date. One of them was in Las Vegas which I insisted we should visit as we were so close, though George wasn't keen. He was probably right as it really struck us an awful place in terms of its values, though aesthetically it had its attractions in the form of fine landscaping in imitation of such iconic places as the Eiffel Tower and the Venetian canals. Its least attractive aspect was the presence of so many children; they were not allowed to gamble but many must have concluded *so this is what you do when you grow up!*

A journey of this length inevitably left a good many memories but some were quite special. One was my relationship with trees. I have always had a strong affinity with them, and in the earlier stages of our journey - southern California, a corner of Arizona - I became aware of a sense of deprivation as we passed through vast areas of semi-desert. Then we crossed over mountains into Nevada, back into forestland and I felt distinctly more at ease.

Thereafter, the landscapes were mixed until we came into the coastal areas of the Pacific where trees take on a whole new meaning. In the shape of redwoods and giant sequoias we are talking of trees that did not merely go back centuries but millennia. It was the giant sequoia I particularly fell for and I have a photograph of George trying to hug one on the screen of my computer. In fact we calculated we would have needed 10-15 Georges to be able successfully to link arms round its massive trunk. At a forest reserve I bought a packet of giant sequoia seeds to take home. In due course, a friend at the Woodland Trust warned "You do realise that if they grow, their roots will cover a square kilometre and cause your village to subside", so perhaps it was as well they didn't.

This particular forest reserve had a number of amazing trees, but the one that impressed me the most was measuring its length on the forest floor, announcing itself to be over 3000 years old (*3,000!!*) so that it had already been more than venerable at the time of Christ's birth. Nor was it dead. It was providing an environment for a host of insects and vegetation including new shoots for its own future generations, not to mention its own new life.

We were able to buy a pass that let us in to most of the State or Federal Reserves. We missed the Grand Canyon but a little later, in Colorado, visited the Black Canyon of the Gunnison, said to be half the depth of the Grand Canyon but quite deep enough and probably more user-friendly. Close to the Canadian border, we drove through part of Montana's Glacier National Park and as we travelled south through California we turned inland to Yosemite where the mountaineer in George had him glued to his binoculars as he scanned a sheer rock face in search of climbers. And found them.

"They would have had to overnight on that climb," he informed me which, as far as I could see, meant hanging by your fingernails for the night hours. Well, it takes all sorts.

On the Californian coast some of the signposting made an impression. One notice, for example, read 'you are entering a tsunami area' while a little further on we were informed we were leaving a tsunami area. And then we remembered how amazed we had been during the tragic Indian Ocean tsunami of Boxing Day 2004 to learn that its effects were felt as far afield as the Californian coast. Other impressive notices were on major buildings in some communities warning that the building had not been strengthened against earthquakes, the implication being that you entered at your own risk!

----oOo----

It was in the early years of the 21st century that Nick, George's youngest son, separated from his wife and in due course was remarried to Paula. But of major international import were two events which occurred within a month of our return from the U.S. The first was the awarding of the Olympics to London for 2012 on 6th July 2005. The second was the terrorist attack in London which followed the next day.

George had gone shopping and a comment on the radio prompted me to switch on the television. The screen showed London streets filled with stricken people, some covered in blood, some standing immovably bewildered. It seemed there had been a bomb explosion first on one underground train, then on another and finally aboard a bus. Much of the rest of the day was spent following the events.

New York, Madrid, London - where next? And that was excluding the innumerable attacks on communities in Afghanistan, Iraq, Pakistan, not to mention the ones of which we never knew. In the years following the Iraq War an increasingly powerful terrorist group developed in the Middle East to become known in the West as al-Qaeda, initially founded by the Jordanian jihadist al-Zarqaur. Also better known in the West was its subsequent leader, Osama bin Laden whose name became synonymous with cruelty of the worst kind throughout the world, but especially in the Middle East against the Shias and in Afghanistan. I have to say that I have always found (and continue to find) the violent discord between Sunni and Shia difficult to understand, unless perhaps applying similar arguments to the bitter divisions in the Christian church in earlier centuries. It was not long before the strengthened group renamed itself the Islamic State of Iraq (ISI) and pledged to "rid Sunnis from the oppression of the (Shia) rejectionists."

Happily there were also some more positive aspects to 2005, one of which was our decision to celebrate Daeda's Wood tenth birthday the following year. It had truly flourished, and we decided to publish a book describing the events leading to its birth and its progress over the ten years. It was decided to call it *A Diary of Daeda's Wood.* I wrote the diary part of it, and other contributions came from various members of the Friends, the Woodland Trust, and local experts.

Above all, much to my surprise, a lot of people who had read *Another Kind of Loving* began asking. "So what happened to Minkie after 9/11?" For some reason, it hadn't occurred to me that a sequel might be required, but the more I thought about it, the more enthusiastic I became about the possibility it would offer to go into more detail about both world wars. So, over the next two years I developed my ideas which resulted, in 2007, in the publication of *Beyond the Broken Gate,* and, finally, in 2010, the third and last in that series, *Long Shadows.*

During this period computer technology sped ahead, becoming ever more versatile, complex, addictive - and prone to error. It provided huge advantages in enabling us to acquire information at the click of a mouse; likewise check our spelling, our mathematics, our bank balances, transfer our money. The possibilities seemed infinite. Clever people of evil intent began to learn how to hack into systems with devastating results. Likewise mobile phones became more versatile, complex, addictive, eventually turning themselves into smartphones that became smarter and smarter until you could do almost as much on them as on a computer. A generation grew into screen addicts.

It was time to re-invent the wheel. Those concerned with our welfare began to urge us to practise ways of learning to live in the here and now. They called it mindfulness, and it was precisely what had been practised in the Far East five or six thousand years earlier.

Back in the present something dramatic and unexpected happened in 2008. A Fellowship friend had come for coffee. One minute we were chatting and the next I was on the floor and she was standing over me, looking anxious.

"I kept shouting at you *don't do this to me*," she kept repeating.

Then George's voice, "What the devil's going on," and there he was, laden with shopping, stricken-faced.

My friend was explaining that I appeared to go into a fit, when I must have drifted off again, because I was next aware of lying in the Assessment Ward at Banbury's Horton Hospital having already had a brain scan. Someone came to ask if I wanted the good or the bad news first. Apparently the bad news was that I had a brain tumour and the good that it was almost certainly benign. It turned out that I had a small growth on the lining of the brain called a meningioma. After an interval in Banbury's Horton Hospital, I was sent to the new neurological department of the John Radcliffe Hospital in Oxford. I have to say that the prospect of a brain op was somewhat alarming, but I clutched a nurse's hand while they put me under and came to gasping for a drink before I knew anything else. The main nuisance was that I could not drive for a year.

Our travels were therefore somewhat restricted by this, and then, equally unexpectedly though not as dramatically, by an event in George's health. It was in the autumn of 2008 that one of my Fellowship friends returned me home from a meeting and, as usual, I let myself into the house through the side door. I awaited the usual greeting of "Aaah, ... it's been so lonely and s-o-o-o-o long", but it didn't come. Instead there was a mumble that was incomprehensible. I went into the living room where George sat in his usual chair looking hunched and uncomfortable.

"I can't move."

"What do you mean, you can't move?"

He proceeded to demonstrate his point, managed to straighten himself a couple of inches but with a pronounced groan of pain. I approached to examine the situation more closely. It looked as though one side of him had seized up. Thoughts of a minor stroke flashed uncomfortably through my mind. "You'll have cramp," I said. "I'll make a cup of tea."

Forty-five minutes later with little obvious change in the situation, we started the arduous business of going to bed. It took a long time. A visit to the surgery next day diagnosed possible hip damage. Some uncomfortable investigations in hospital confirmed there was no hip problem, and the diagnosis settled on polymyalgia rheumatica. We learned this could occur with little warning, especially among older people.

A helpful physiotherapist came to assess the situation and recommend various aids, including a picker-upper which George delighted in using to retrieve the objects he kept dropping. He was also provided with a walking frame which would have been even more helpful if he had not always abandoned it in the hall.

It was at about this time that modern technology imposed upon us even smarter phones. I never did manage to master it and have probably become one of the few people not to possess one. Indeed modern communications, presumably intended to make life easier, have made it far more complicated since it is almost impossible to talk to a real human. In addition humans, of almost any age, seem to prefer to talk to someone far away on their mobile rather than whomever is with them at the time.

Now that we were both more Deddington-bound, I felt we both needed to take a look at our social lives. George had never been terribly sociable outside the mountaineering-canoeing-camping-reading worlds. He did, however, enjoy his wine and, since I'd stopped drinking alcohol, this had also restricted him rather. My social life was largely involved with the Fellowship and I was still to some extent involved in village activities. George had acquired the habit of joining a small wine-drinking group in one of the central village pubs every Wednesday evening, walking in and then I would pick him up an hour or two later. When I couldn't drive, one of the members of the group brought him back.

The prospects of foreign travel did not seem good until our Finnish friends came to the rescue. "We think it would be a good idea," Matti said on the phone, "if you plan to spend Juhannus with us next year." *Juhannus* is what the Finns call Midsummer, and is a holiday when nearly all Finland goes to the countryside to enjoy days that are up to twenty-four hours long. Matti planned that we should travel with their car on the train to Rovaniemi on the Arctic Circle and then drive to a self-catering summer cottage way up in Lapland. It was grand to have something to look forward to during our rather static winter.

By now George had considerably cut back on his winter lecture tours. Now in his mid-eighties, long drives and frequent nights in the car were no longer as appealing; and many schools and societies had moved on to sophisticated new technology. Instead he did more W.I. bookings, which did not pay as well but kept his hand in and gave him an opportunity to share his experiences. When he started cutting back on W.I. talks, I began to wonder whether I might have a try .

The potential talk I found most appealing because it was so full of anecdotes was our canoe trip down the Mississippi. I began by creating a dossier of coloured photographs that illustrated various stages of our journey, and provided a map so that people could follow our progress. It was quite time-taking as I needed 12-15 sets to share out among the average local W.I. audience, but it proved worthwhile and everyone seemed to appreciate the sets of photographs that they could look back on as they wished. As a new speaker, I had to go through an audition, but I did and succeeded, so well into my seventies embarked on a new career! At least having attended many of George's talks, I had picked up a good few hints. Later I added another talk, based on our experience with Servas and staying in private homes during our marathon drive through the western U.S.; and later still devised a talk based on my writing career. It turned out to provide an excellent additional opportunity for selling books.

So we prepared for our midsummer trip to northern Finland. I noted that, with the stimulus of new surroundings, George's inclination to walk increased. Our friends were committed to Helsinki for a couple more days and left us to our own devices and we, and especially George, walked miles. And so on to the train for our overnight journey to the Arctic Circle where we arrived, to everyone's astonishment, in a gentle flurry of snow!

It was about a two hour's drive to 'our' cottage. It was grand to be in the far north after so long and, though communities had grown, I had forgotten quite how gloriously empty most of Lapland was. The cottage was lovely: very well equipped and a few yards from the lake shore on which there was a sauna. We went to explore and stood looking out across the lake. A small boat crossed the water in the distance. "This place is getting so crowded," I said. Matti looked at me, recognised the irony and grinned.

We had a wonderful week there, including visits to haunts not seen for decades. These included Pallastunturi where I had taught English in 1960, now mainly an excellent information centre. We did a walk to the top of one of the local fells and it was good to see George reach the summit rather more quickly than I did. And, of course, because it was midsummer, the daylight hours stretched to twenty-four hours long. All in all our trip to Finland did him a power of good. He wasn't exactly ready to go back to the gym, but he started attending YRC week-ends again, and there was a noticeable lifting of his spirits.

And then one week-end he set off for Yorkshire in spite of complaining of a chest pain. On the Saturday evening one of his friends rang. "George isn't too good. Don't worry - he's coming back

179

with us tomorrow. He's been checked over but we don't think he should be driving. Two of us are travelling back to Oxford together, so one will drive George back in your car and I'll drive mine."

I was so grateful for the common sense of these friends, especially when it transpired that George had had a pulmonary embolism. And so the prescription of warfarin and the regular checks associated with it entered our lives.

We were not the only couple for whom age was bringing major health concerns. Our good friend Norman Stone had developed cancer some time earlier; it had spread and after some months of harrowing decline, he died in the summer of 2010. I felt deeply for his wife Angela for we were both 'second wives' without our own children.

But terminal illness was not our only concern that year. In December 2010, a stallholder in Tunis set fire to himself in protest at government action. It triggered a wave of public unrest in the Middle East which became known as the Arab Spring, overturning the rulers of Tunisia and Egypt and triggering revolt in Libya which had become a military dictatorship under Gaddafi. What gave rise to initial hopes of a new era of political tolerance was short lived, and in the following years, the worst kind of intolerance was spawned by fundamentalism of the greatest intransigence in no small measure resulting from the thoughtless creation of borders after World War One. The worst excesses continued to be between the Sunnis and Shias, perpetrated in particular by the former. Nor did the situation in Palestine improve with the building of a security wall to contain the West Bank and reduce the number of suicide bombs.

Then, in July 2011, I suffered another major loss when my sister Sinette died in Australia. She had recently returned from a holiday with Claire at Nick's in New South Wales and had gone to hospital for a check up. While there she went to the loo and dropped dead and her known wishes that she should not be resuscitated were respected.

I thought she had forgotten to telephone me that morning but, no, next morning Claire rang me to tell me the news. Though we spoke regularly on the phone, we hadn't seen each other for quite a while so, initially, her absence did not impinge. But she had always been there since Day One, sometimes a bit bossy but nearly always with a lot of common sense. And I gradually realised that I really was the last one standing. Life began to feel lonely. This may have been accentuated by the fact that for some time I had been aware that

George was either becoming forgetful or more inattentive. It became a regular occurrence for me to tell him in the morning what I was doing in the afternoon, only to be told that he hadn't been informed when I announced I was going out.

Last tomorrow

When I mentioned George's erratic memory to his G.P., she arranged for him to have a basic memory test at the surgery. He didn't do too badly, but it was suggested he should attend the Memory Clinic in Oxford where, towards the end of 2011, they diagnosed early stages of dementia, prescribed medication, and suggested I got power of attorney for managing our basic affairs. Increasingly I noticed how often George asked a question and very soon forgot the answer. With help from Age UK, we successfully applied for the Attendance Allowance which was a great boon in getting a carer several mornings a week to help George shower and dress allowing me to get on with household chores. She was not only helpful but a sweetie who helped brighten his mornings.

For some time I had also been a little concerned about his driving. He had , in fact, had a driving test some time earlier at the instigation of our doctor and passed without a problem. But I had become conscious of his lack of awareness, especially at roundabouts, towards traffic overtaking from the outside. In the end the decision was taken for us.

Towards the end of May, I decided to take a table in the church at Deddington's Farmers' Market and see if I could interest anyone in my newest book, *The Other Side of Silence.* This was based on Finland, its participation in World War Two, and it incorporated a lot that I had learned about that country over the years, as well as some of George's flying and p.o.w. experience. The only problem was that I needed the car in order to get the books to the church, which meant that George would have to drive it back home.

Anyway, he unloaded me and my trolley-load of books near the church and I watched him drive off a bit jerkily towards home. As I manoeuvred the trolley into the church, someone grabbed me. "You'd better check on George. He seems to have driven into the Deddington Arms ."

And there the car was with its bonnet buried in a broken bay window and George still in the driver's seat, looking bewildered. "I don't know what happened," he kept repeating. We wouldn't let him move until the paramedics arrived. The police came first, then the fire brigade to move the car which was blocking part of the road, and finally the paramedics who pronounced that George had cracked his sternum and some ribs and should be taken to A&E.

"Oh my God!" Adrian groaned when I rang to give the news.

"I'll be over at the week-end," Julian said.

Adrian was the first to come over. We drove over to the police pound where written off cars are dumped, and emptied the car of anything worth taking. Julian rang to say he'd found a garage near Coventry which had a nice-sounding Skoda for sale. Within a week it was ours.

The main damage to George was the pain in his sternum while it repaired, cracked ribs and wounded pride. It took a while for him to understand that he could no longer drive: *why?* (because you lost your licence); *why?* (because you crashed the car); *when?* (when you drove into the Deddington Arms); pause. *Oh yes, so I did, didn't I!* Until the next forgetting.

I began increasingly to think how sensible it would be to move into the middle of the village. Not only was George's walking limited but so was that of the ageing friends he might want to meet. When I mentioned it, he was distinctly unenthusiastic.

"What about my books?" he said.

Yes, that could be a problem for there were a great many of them. But we no longer needed two offices and there should be a way round it.

And then he started falling down rather a lot. He didn't tell me about the early falls, but in due course found he couldn't get up. Neighbours were helpful but then it became necessary to call the paramedics which I always rather dreaded for if they had any suspicion that something needed more than their expertise, it meant a visit to A&E and usually a very long wait until the required tests could take place. Otherwise they (the paramedics) were truly marvellous. About this time he developed an ulcer on his ankle, notoriously difficult to get rid of when you are old. It needed dressing two or three times a week at the surgery. All the same we planned a visit to the north of England that summer. George needed to see his friends, and we both needed something to plan.

In the meantime the memory loss was increasing and he had acquired a walker to help him get round the house. Invariably the latter ended up in the wrong place so in due course we acquired a second walker so that we could have one upstairs and one down. It was still usually in the wrong place but it was not so far to go and retrieve it

The Arab Spring continued to unfold more like a disastrous winter, as millions of innocent people were displaced and hundreds of thousands died from conflicts, disease or hunger, and sprawling refugee camps burgeoned in some of Europe's poorer countries. To these were added an increasing number of Africans mostly arriving from Libya to seek a better life in Europe. Many perished in overladen vessels for which they paid exorbitant fees to unscrupulous people-smugglers. By now ISI had joined with another group to form the Islamic State of Iraq and the Levant (ISIL) and became major players in the disastrous civil war of Syria, eventually declaring itself to be a worldwide caliphate and thus the ultimate authority over Moslems globally.

While I brooded on this, we planned our trip to the north of England, beginning with a few nights at the Club hut near Clapham in Yorkshire, then booking ourselves in for bed and breakfast in the village where Tom Price and his partner Jean lived. It was good to meet a number of George's climbing friends and for him to be able to relax in settings that had been such a major part of his life.

I remember watching an unusual amount of sport on television that summer, for that was the summer of the Olympics and Paralympics in London. George watched too but usually fell asleep. Julian and Adrian especially visited us; Julian and Marilyn were planning to move out of Bristol and indeed did so just before Christmas, finding a house in a village in Shropshire. I kept in touch with local estate agents and in due course found a two-bedroom flat with reasonable wall space in the centre of Deddington. After some careful measuring I concluded we could fit in most of George's books, and when he saw it and how conveniently it was placed for several pubs where he could meet his friends, he began to consider the idea of a move.

Over the next week or two I played with measuring furniture and plans; it was clearly going to be a tight fit, but not impossible. A quiet Christmas came and went. I was feeling a bit drained by the events of the past months and, on a visit to m G.P., she told me that, with all his health issues, it was not likely that George would see the end of 2013. I'm not sure I took it seriously. He had survived so many dramas and, even now when I expressed concern about him, he gave me that grin of his and said, "Oh don't worry, it'll be better tomorrow."

We learned that Paul, Julian's son from his first marriage, had become engaged to his long term American girl friend Kim. They were was visiting England and wanted to take us out to lunch early in February. Paul's and Kim's visit was a pleasant occasion. Paul was continuing to commute between Sydney and New York with his advanced technology, and Kim seemed a very pleasant young lady with a great interest in George's background.

In the mean time George had finally agreed to a move and I asked our solicitor to come on the evening of February 13th to discuss procedures for putting our house on the market. George said that he was glad I was in charge as he didn't think he would remember it all. Once the solicitor had left I began putting together a light supper during which I heard an unexpected exclamation from George, and found him leaning far forward over his knees in his armchair. He didn't seem able to explain what was wrong so I dialled 999. The paramedics asked several questions, and finally "Ask your husband if he's hurting."

I relayed the question to George who managed to say with difficulty "Not hurting... but very ... very confused." Then he slumped forward further.

They were his last words. The paramedics arrived very soon after, but could not revive him. I rang a close neighbour and friend who was also a rector and he came immediately.

The rest was confusion and paperwork and telephone calls and numbness.

It was a while before I was able to think gratefully how right it had been for George to move on from illness into peace, hopefully without fear and without the hassle of moving house. And how hugely lucky I had been to enjoy such a relationship.

And it was a while more before I eventually asked myself, "**So, what next?**"

For reasons which do not need discussion here, there arose a disagreement with my stepsons, though Julian, the eldest, continues to visit, do useful jobs and give advice. Claire and Nick, my only blood relatives, are in Australia. I was quite ill for a while and spent some weeks in a residential home in Deddington, close enough to my flat to be able to divide my time between the two. Depression combined with bereavement is not a lot of fun, not helped by the death of several of my and George's friends in the following months.

Over the next three years, I moved twice: initially to the flat in Deddington, the second time into the town of Banbury in order to be closer to amenities I may well need in due course, join groups that might provide an intellectual challenge, and be more closely involved with the Fellowship. More friends died. I learned of the death of Sveto, my academic Serb friend, through the Internet. Others I have just had to assume as they completely disappeared from my Radar, including work colleagues and childhood friends.

As someone said, 'Old age is not for cissies.' They were dead right. But I did my best. I brought out my first book for Young Adults, *Courage to Change,* on overcoming addiction. I made a trip to Switzerland to take family documents that needed to be archived, some dating back to World War One. I also wrote an anthology of short stories named after George's favourite saying *It'll be Better Tomorrow.* And I celebrated my 85th birthday in Australia, a day after Nick's sixtieth and Claire's fifty-seventh. By then Nick and Greg had moved to a delightful place west of Sydney, near Greg's parents and were taking up sheep farming. It was interesting to learn that a previous owner of the house they had bought was a cousin of Winston Churchill, buried in a nearby churchyard. A photograph of him confirmed his family connection though I was unable to find anything else about him on the Internet.

The family and I plan to re-unite in 2020 in Australia for my 90th, Nicks's 65th and Claire's 61st birthdays.

At home, younger members of the Fellowship became godsends in treating me like a batty old aunt and filling some of the void left by the loss of my best mate and lack of family. Above all, I decided to write this account of my - and George's - experience of modern times leading up to perhaps the most troubled time in history. Since his death Julian's son Paul married his Kim and, altogether, George has so far acquired five great grandchildren; I hope they and later descendants will enjoy learning about their special ancestor.

And there may yet be another book in due course. A mystery begins to appeal, with someone suffering from dementia as the hero. Having lived with it, I know the real person is still there beyond the illness, and deserves continued recognition.

Acknowledgments

I'm profoundly grateful to all those who have contributed to a deeply enjoyable life. In particular I am grateful to my family. They say you can't choose your family, but I don't think I could possibly have fared better given all the choice in the world.

And then I am deeply grateful to my husband and best mate, George Spenceley, with whom I shared so many interests, nearly four decades of marriage, and who had the gift of empathy for the incomprehensible moods that go with depression.

Thank you to Alison Day for helping me to check the manuscript and save me from some embarrassing mistakes; and in due course, with endless patience, turn an eBook into this paperback. Thank you Paul Cowpland and family for being such a support in both practical and companionable ways. Thank you to the Deddington Writers Group and the help provided by their comments over a number of years - in particular Norman Stone and, by association, his wife Angela. Thank you to the staff and residents of Featherton House in Deddington who eased the pain of bereavement, some of whom provided material for an anthology of short stories. Special thanks to the Fellowship through whom recovery from addiction changed my life. And thanks to Brian Tabor whose financial advice made life manageable for my remaining time.

And thank you, world, for being such an interesting place. I hope you manage to get yourself sorted out from the mess some of us have made of you.

Lightning Source UK Ltd.
Milton Keynes UK
UKHW03f0321140418
321053UK00001B/44/P